W

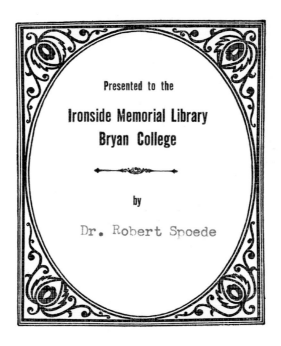

Presented to the

**Ironside Memorial Library
Bryan College**

by

Dr. Robert Spoede

DISCOURSES ON DAVILA

A Da Capo Press Reprint Series

STUDIES IN AMERICAN HISTORY AND GOVERNMENT

GENERAL EDITOR: LEONARD W. LEVY

Claremont Graduate School

DISCOURSES ON DAVILA

A Series of Papers on Political History

By John Adams

DA CAPO PRESS • NEW YORK • 1973

51884

Library of Congress Cataloging in Publication Data

Adams, John, Pres. U.S., 1735-1826.
  Discourses on Davila.

  (Studies in American history and government)
  Reprint of the 1805 ed.
  1. Davila, Enrico Caterino, 1576-1631. Historia
delle guerre civili di Francia. 2. France-History—
Wars of the Huguenots, 1502-1598. 3. Political
science. I. Title.
JK171.A23   1973   944'.029   70-87665
ISBN 0-306-71761-1

This Da Capo Press edition of *Discourses on Davila*
is an unabridged republication of the
1805 edition published in Boston.

Da Capo Press, Inc.
A Subsidiary of Plenum Publishing Corporation
227 West 17th Street, New York, New York 10011

All Rights Reserved

Manufactured in the United States of America

DISCOURSES ON DAVILA

DISCOURSES

ON

D A V I L A.

A SERIES OF PAPERS,

ON

POLITICAL HISTORY.

WRITTEN IN THE YEAR 1790, AND THEN PUBLISHED IN THE

GAZETTE OF THE UNITED STATES.

BY AN AMERICAN CITIZEN.

NON PONEBAT RUMORES ANTE SALUTEM.

" Truths would you teach, to fave a finking land,
" All read, none aid you, and few underftand.
" 'Twas then the ftudious head, or gen'rous mind,
" Foll'wer of God, or friend of human kind,
" Taught Pow'rs due ufe to people and to kings,
" Taught nor to flack nor ftrain its tender ftrings
" The lefs or greater, fet fo juftly true,
" That touching one muft ftrike the other too ;
" Till jaring interefts, of themfelves, create
" Th' according mufic of a well mix'd State.
" Such is the world's great harmony that fprings
" From order, union, full confent of things ;
" Where fmall and great, where weak and mighty made
" To ferve, not fuffer—ftrengthen, not invade ;
" More powerful each, as needful to the reft,
" And in proportion as it bleñes, bleft......................POPE.

BOSTON,
PRINTED BY RUSSELL AND CUTLER.
1805.

ADVERTISEMENT.

THE Numbers, which form this Vol. were originally publifhed in the Gazette of the United States, at New-York and Philadelphia, during the year 1790 ; and were then fuppofed to be the production of the celebrated author of the " *Defence of the American Conftitutions.*" In fupport of this opinion, we could, if it were neceffary, give many reafons ; but the reader, on a careful perufal of them, will readily difcover, that they are the offspring of the fame mind, and may be diftinctly confidered as correlative parts, or an *additional volume* to the above work. With this view we have been governed, both in the fize of the type and page, and in the quality of the paper, to the American edition of the *Defence.*

THE EDITORS.

PREFACE.

SINCE the publication of thefe Difcourfes in 1790, our obfervations abroad, and experience at home, have fufficiently taught us the leffons they were intended to inculcate ; and the evils they were defigned to prevent, have borne teftimony of their truth.

It is unneceffary to mention the rank or reputation of the fuppofed author, to give celebrity to the work. The Difcourfes are allowed, by the beft judges, to form a complete effay on affociated man, in which practical improvement is drawn from profound inveftigation ; his principles of action, as an individual, traced to their effects in his relative capacity ; and from the light of hiftory, and a thorough knowledge of his nature, his paft difafters are made fubfervient to his prefent and future happinefs.

The maxims inculcated in thefe Difcourfes, are calculated to fecure virtue, by laying a reftraint upon vice ; to give vigour and durability to the tree of liberty, by pruning its excrefcencies ; and to guard it againft the tempeft of faction, by the protection of a firm and well-balanced government.

A work, combining fo much excellence, on a fubject of fuch dignity and importance, cannot be too much appreciated........ Conceiving it to be both ufeful and honorable to their country the Editors are defirous of preferving it from the inevitable wreck of a newfpaper publication ; and believing the work will not fail of being approved by their fellow-citizens, they now tranfmit it to the public in a more durable form, without the aid of fubfcription or private patronage.

———

Two Factions, drunk with Enthufiafm, and headed by men of the moft defperate Ambition, defolated France.

Remarks on the Hiftory of England.

Bofton, March, 1805.

DISCOURSES ON DAVILA.

No. 1.

Fœlix, quem faciunt aliena pericula cautum.

THE French nation, known in antiquity under the appellation of the Franks, were originally from the heart of Germany. In the declenfion of the Roman Empire, they inhabited a country in the North, along the river Rhine, fituated between Bavaria and Saxony, which ftill preferves the name of Franconia. Having exceffively multiplied, as it happens in cold climates, their country was found not fufficiently extenfive to contain them, nor fertile enough to nourifh them. Excited by the example of their neighbours, they refolved, by a common voice, to divide themfelves into two nations; one of which fhould continue to inhabit their antient country; and the other endeavour to procure, elfewhere, by the force of arms, an eftablifhment more vaft, more commodious, and more fertile. This enterprife was refolved, and this divifion made by unanimous confent. Such as were deftined by lot, to effay their fortune, although trained to war, and incapable of terror, at the apprehenfion of the dangers of fuch an enterprife, thought, however, that they ought not to abandon it to anarchy or hazard, but to conduct it with prudence and order. To concert the

B   meafures

meafures neceffary for the execution of their project, they affembled in the plains, in the neighbourhood of the river *Sala.* Accuftomed for many ages, to live in the obedience of a Prince, and thinking the monarchical ftate the moft convenient to a people who afpire to augment their power, and extend their conquefts, they refolved to choofe a King, who fhould unite in his fingle perfon, *all the authority of the nation.* Here perhaps DAVILA is incautious and incorrect; for the Franks, as well as Saxons, and other German nations, though their governments were monarchical, had their Grandees and People, who met and deliberated in National Affemblies, whofe refults were often, to fay the leaft, confidered as laws. Their great misfortune was, that, while it never was fufficiently afcertained, whether the fovereignty refided in the King, or in the *National Affembly,* it was equally uncertain, whether the King had a negative on the affembly; whether the Grandees had a negative on the King, or the people; and whether the people had a negative on both, or either. This uncertainty will appear hereafter, in DAVILA himfelf, to mark its courfe in bloody characters; and the whole hiftory of France will fhew, that from the firft migration of the Franks from Germany to this hour, it has never been fufficiently explained and decided.

To this fupreme degree of power in the King (as DAVILA proceeds) they added, that the *crown* fhould be *hereditary* in the family elected; forefeeing, that if it were *elective,* it would be a fource of civil wars, which would prove deftructive to all their enterprifes. Mankind, in new eftablifhments, generally act with fincerity, and with a fingle view to the public good. They lif-

ten

ten neither to the ambition nor the interest of private persons : Pharamond was elected King, by unanimous consent. He was a son of Marcomir, issue of the blood which had governed the nation for many ages ; and, to an experienced valor, united a profound wisdom, in the art of government. It was agreed that the same title, and equal power, should descend to his legitimate posterity of the male line, in default of which the nation should return to their right of electing a new sovereign. But as unlimited authority may easily degenerate into tyranny, the Franks, at the time of the election of their King, demanded the establishment of certain perpetual and irrevocable laws, which should regulate the order of succession to the throne, and prescribe in a few words, the form of government. These laws, proposed by their priests, whom they named *Saliens*, and instituted in the fields, which take their name from the river *Sala*, were originally called *Salique laws*, and have been considered, from the establishment of the monarchy, as the primitive regulations and fundamental constitutions of the kingdom.

Leaving their country to the old Prince Marcomir, and passing the Rhine, under the command of Pharamond, the Franks marched to the conquest of the Gauls, about the four hundred and nineteenth year of the christian Æra. The Roman legions, united with the Gaulish troops, resisted Pharamond, till his death. The sceptre was left to his son Clodion, an intrepid Prince, in the flower of his age, who in several battles defeated the nations of the country, dissipated the Roman armies, and established himself in Belgick Gaul. Merovius, who succeeded him, made a rapid progress ; penetrated into Celtic Gaul,

and

and extended his empire to the gates of Paris ; judging that he had conquered country enough to contain his fubjects, and form a ftate of reafonable extent, he limited the courfe of his exploits, and turned all his cares to peace, after having united under the fame laws, and the fame name, the conquerors and the vanquifhed, whom he governed peaceably. He died leaving the Franks folidly eftablifhed in Gaul : Such is the origin of the French monarchy, and fuch are her fundamental laws.

By the difpofitions of the fame laws, the work of the nation, are regulated, the rights and prerogatives of the Princes of the Blood : As each of them, in default of direct heirs, may, according to his rank, be called to the crown, their interefts are neceffarily connected with thofe of the ftate. The people regard thefe privileges, as inviolable : Neither length of time, nor diftance of degree has ever done them any injury. All thefe Princes preferve the rank which nature has allotted them, to fucceed to the throne. They have indeed, in the courfe of time, taken different names, fuch as thofe of *Valois,* of *Bourbons,* of *Orleans,* of *Angouleme,* of *Vendome,* of *Alencon,* of *Montpenfier ;* but they have not by thefe means loft the rights attached to the royal confanguinity, that, efpecially of fucceeding to the crown. Thefe different branches, have from time to time afferted the pre-eminence, due to their blood ; to intereft them the more forcibly, in the prefervation of a crown, to which, in fucceffion, they may all be called, it has been commonly made a rule, in cafe of the minority, or abfence of the lawful King, to choofe for the tutors or regents of the kingdom, the Princes who were neareft related ; it would not indeed be natural to entruft the adminiftration miniſtration to the hands of ſtrangers, who might deſtroy, or at leaſt diſmember ſo beautiful a ſtate : Whereas Princes born of the ſame blood, ought, for that reaſon, to watch over the conſervation of an inheritance, which belongs to them, in ſome ſort.   This right is not ſimply founded upon uſage : The *States General* of the Kingdom, in whom reſides the entire power of the whole nation whom they repreſent, have frequently confirmed it.—Here again we meet with another inaccuracy, if not a contradiction in DAVILA ; or rather with another proof of that confuſion of law, and that uncertainty of the ſovereignty, which for 1500 years has been to France, the fatal ſource of ſo many calamities :* Here the ſovereignty, or whole power of the nation, is aſſerted to be in the *ſtates general ;* whereas only three pages before, he had aſſerted that the whole authority of the nation was united in the King.

Theſe two prerogatives, of ſucceeding to the throne when a King dies without maſculine poſterity, and of governing the kingdom during the abſence or minority of the legitimate ſovereign, have at all times procured to the Princes of the blood, a great authority among the people, and the beſt part in the government.   They have applied themſelves accordingly with remarkable vigilance, to the adminiſtration of an Empire, which they regarded with juſtice as their patrimony : And the people, judging that they might have them one day for their firſt Magiſtrates, have always ſhewn them the more reſpect, as they have more than once known the younger branches to aſcend the Throne, in default of the elder. Thus the Crown has paſſed from the Merovingians

* Misera Servitus est, ubi jus est vagum aut incognitum. 1804.

gians to the Carlovingians, and finally to the
Capetians ; but always from male to male, in
the Princes of the blood of thefe three races.
From the laft of thefe defcended the King Louis
the eleventh, whom the innocence of his life and
the integrity of his manners, have placed in the
number of the Saints. He left two fons, Philip
the third, furnamed the Hardy ; and Robert, Earl
of Clermont. Philip continued the elder branch,
which reigned more than three hundred years,
and took the furname of Valois. From Robert
is defcended the younger branch, or the houfe of
Bourbon, fo called, from the province, in which
it poffeffed its fettlement. This houfe, refpectable not only by birth, which placed it near the
throne, but alfo by the extent of its lands and
riches, by the valour and number of its Princes,
almoft all diftinguifhed by their merit and a fingular affability, arrived foon at an high degree
of power. This elevation, joined to the favour
of the people, excited againft the Bourbons, the
jealoufy and envy of the Kings, whom this great
credit and diftinguifhed fplendor, difpleafed, and
alarmed. Every day brought frefh occafions of
hatred, fufpicion and diftruft, which feveral times
broke out in arms. Thus in the war, *for the
public good*, John, Duke of Bourbon, declared himfelf againft Louis the eleventh ; and Louis the
twelfth, before his acceffion to the throne, was at
war with Peter of Bourbon. The jealoufies
which thefe Princes infpired into Kings, expofed
them fometimes to fecret vexations, and fometimes to declared enmities. We may add to this
reflection of Davila, that it is extremely probable, that thefe Princes, by frequently betraying
fymptoms of ambition, afpiring at the throne,
might give to Kings, juft grounds of jealoufy
and alarm.   Before

Before we proceed in our difcourfes on DAVI-LA, it will affift us, in comprehending his narration, as well as in making many ufeful reflections in morals and policy, to turn our thoughts for a few moments to the conftitution of the human mind. This we fhall endeavour to do in our next effay.

No. 2.

La nature parle aux cœurs des Rois, tout comme a ceux des particuliers.

NATURE fpeaks the fame language to the hearts of Princes, as to thofe of other men. Kings compare themfelves with Kings, or with fuch of their own fubjects, as are neareft to them ; and have the fame fentiments as private perfons, of pride, vanity, jealoufy, refentment, and hatred, arifing from fuch comparifons.

FRANCIS Ift. after his afcenfion to the throne, whether he was mifled by an imprudence of youth, or whether he confulted only his own beneficent difpofition, propofed to himfelf, from the firft day of his reign, to aggrandize the Princes of the blood, and load them with favours. To elevate in dignity thofe who belonged to the Royal family, by proximity of blood, he believed to be for his own glory. Having difcerned in *Charles,* the head of the branch of Bourbon, all the talents which form the great Captain, and the able Statesman, he gave him the office of Conftable ; and by confering on him, and the Princes of that houfe, the moft diftinguifhed employments, he placed them at the head of the moft important affairs

of

of his kingdom.* This it muſt be confeſſed was impolitic ; ſince it is always dangerous for the firſt in office or command, to be over fond or familiar with the ſecond—to confer too many opportunities of eclipſing his own glory, or of drawing away the attention of the public ; or to offer too many temptations to ambition, rivalry, or envy. Accordingly the firſt fire of this zeal abated ; and experience having excited his jealouſy, or policy revealed to him the reaſons of the conduct. which his predeceſſors had holden ; he manifeſted in the ſequel as much eagerneſs to lower the Bourbons, as he had at firſt diſcovered of affection to exalt them.

Fortune ſoon preſented an opportunity favorable to his deſign. Louiſa of Savoy, his mother, had commenced a law ſuit againſt Charles, for the Dutchy of Bourbon, in his poſſeſſion. *Judges, in thoſe days, were not independent.*—The King thought that by influencing the deciſion, in favor of his mother, and by thus deſpoiling the houſe of Bourbon of the richeſt portion of their patrimony, he might accelerate the declenſion of a credit, founded in part on their immenſe riches.—Charles, in the courſe of the proceedings, diſcovered the manœuvres, which were practiſed to his prejudice, by the Chancellor Duprat, by order of the King. The indignation, which he conceived at this injury, and the apprehenſion of the reverſe of fortune which threatened him, ſtruck him ſo forcibly, that, having negociated ſecretly with the Emperor, Charles the fifth, and Henry the eighth, King of England, he conſpired againſt

---

* See the late correſpondence between the Prince of Wales and his father, brother, &c.—Alſo, reccollect the conduct of the Duke of Malborough and Queen Ann and her Miniſters.—By ſuch combination of circumſtances, what havoc is made with conſtitutions and adminiſtrations.—1804.

againſt the State, and even againſt the perſon of the King. His deſigns were diſcovered ; and, neceſſiated to fly the kingdom with precipitation, he afterwards bore arms againſt his ſovereign.— He commanded the Imperial army at the battle of Pavia, in which, after the bloody defeat of the French army, the King furrounded on all ſides by the infantry of the enemy, remained a priſoner. The Conſtable, as a puniſhment of all theſe crimes, was declared a rebel : All his eſtates were confiſcated and united to the dominions of the crown. He was killed ſoon after, at the taking of Rome : and there remained to the Bourbons nothing of that grandeur, which had inſpired ſo much umbrage to Kings. Their misfortunes did not ceaſe here.—Although Charles was deceaſed without iſſue, and the other Princes of his Houſe had not favored his revolt, reſentment in the breaſt of the King overcame his reaſon, and the Bourbons were deprived of the favours of the court, and baniſhed from the government. Their perſonal merit could not ſoften the hatred attached to their name. This rigour, it is true, diminiſhed with time, and in proportion as the memory of the paſt, and the diſadvantageous ideas which the King had conceived of them, were effaced from his mind. Nevertheleſs, he cautiouſly applied himſelf, to obſtruct all the paſſages, by which they might have returned to the poſſeſſion of thoſe dignities, and that power, to which royal favor had formerly raiſed them. Theſe ſecret diſpoſitions of the King were perfectly known to Charles of Vendome, now at the head of that Houſe, who by his moderation, ſtudied to diſſipate the ſuſpicions, which were entertained againſt his family : in this view he refuſed, during the impriſon-

c

ment

ment of the King, to pretend to the regency, which belonged to him, of right.—After the King was fet at liberty, Charles ſhut himſelf up with his domeſtics, leading a private life, without meddling in the government of a State, in which he faw he was fufpected. All the other Bourbons, after his example, retired, as much to prove that they were innocent of the revolt of the Conſtable, as to mark their fubmiſſion to the will of the King, even when it was moſt difadvantageous to them. They avoided every thing which could revive the diſtruſt againſt them ; and, too openly in diſgrace, to think of elevating themfelves to thoſe dignities which they thought alone fuitable to their birth, and too haughty to defcend to the ſmaller places, they renounced all the honors and offices of the court. The fame caufes produce the fame effects. The late revolution in France, opened a profpect to the Royal family, not very different from that in 1515. Though the merits and injuries of Orleans, may not be compared to thofe of a Conſtable de Bourbon ; yet the paſſions of a Prince of the blood of the fecond order may hereafter be painted by another DAVILA. Opportunity will generally excite ambition to afpire ; and if even an improbable cafe ſhould happen of an exception to this rule, danger will always be fufpected and apprehended, in fuch circumftances, from fuch caufes. We may foon fee, that a form of government, in which every paſſion has an adequate counterpoife, can alone fecure the public from the dangers and mifchiefs, of fuch rivalries, jealoufies, envies and hatreds.

Auguſt veritè !
C'eſt a toi, de montrer aux yeux des nations
Les coupables effets de leurs diviſions.

WHEN one family is depreſſed, either in a Monarchy, or in any ſpecies of republic, another muſt ariſe. While, in the reign of FRANCIS Iſt, they thus humbled the branch of the Bourbons ; there aroſe two other powerful families, who ſoon obtained the adminiſtration of affairs : The houſe of *Montmorency*, and that of *Guiſe* ; both, indeed inferior to the Blood Royal ; but both illuſtrious by the ſplendor of the moſt ancient nobility. That of Montmorency produces Titles, which prove its deſcent, by an uninterrupted ſucceſſion, from one of the principal Grandees who accompanied Pharamond in his firſt expedition. It has the glory of having been the firſt French houſe which received baptiſm and the Chriſtian Faith. The memory of this diſtinction is preſerved in the motto of their arms, *God help the firſt Chriſtian Baron* ; a ſplendid teſtimony both of the antiquity and religion of their anceſtors. Anne of Montmorency, who united a vaſt genius, directed by prudence, to a grave and impoſing deportment—who combined a ſingular addreſs to a patience never to be exhauſted in the intrigues and affairs of the Court, which change ſo often their aſpect, ſprung from this ſtock.— His high qualities merited the confidence of Francis Iſt. After having paſſed through all the military gradations of the State, he was at firſt elevated to the dignity of Grand Maſter of the King's houſehold, and after the death of the Duke of of Bourbon, to that of *Conftable*—in one word he concentered in his perfon, the command of armies, and the principal adminiftration of all the affairs, civil and political, of the kingdom.

The houfe of *Lorrain*, of which that of *Guife* is a branch, derives its original, from the higheft antiquity. It reckons among its paternal anceftors, Godfrey of Bouillon, the famous leader of the Crufades, who by his valor and piety conquered the kingdom of Jerufalem ; and by the female line it traces its defcent from a daughter of Charlemain. Anthony, of Lorrain, chief of this rich and powerful family, reigned over his people, with an abfolute authority : Claud, his younger brother, went into France to take pof-feffion of the Dutchy of Guife, and there recommended himfelf by his valor.—After the battle of Marignan, where he commanded the German troops, he was taken out from an heap of dead bodies, covered over with blood and wounds ; his cure was thought to be a miracle, and he held afterwards the firft rank among the greateft captains of France. The houfes of Guife and Montmorency, had rendered fervices of fuch importance to the State that it was difficult to determine, which of the two merited the pre-eminence. In the fplendor of their birth, and the extent of their domains, the Guifes had the advantage.— In the favor of the King, the family of the Conftable was moft advanced, and faw itfelf at the head of affairs. Nature, which has eftablifhed in the univerfe a chain of being and univerfal order, defcending from Arch Angels to microfcopic animalcules, has ordained that no two objects fhall be perfectly alike, and no two creatures perfectly equal. Although among men, all are fubject

ject by nature to *equal laws* of morality, and in
society have a right to *equal laws* for their government, yet no two men are perfectly equal in
perfon, property, underftanding, activity and virtue—or ever can be made fo by any power lefs
than that which created them ; and whenever
it becomes difputable between two individuals,or
families, which is the fuperior, a fermentation
commences,which difturbs the órder of all things,
until it is fettled, and each one knows his place
in the opinion of the public. The queftion of
fuperiority between the Guifes and Montmorencies had the ufual effects of fuch doubts. But
as nothing is lefs ftable than the fortune of courtiers, in ill-ordered governments, they both experienced reverfes, towards the end of the reign
of Francis the Ift. That jealoufy, which never
has an end, becaufe it is always well founded,
which reigns in every government, where every
paffion and every intereft has not its correfpondent counterpoife, actuated the King. The two
minifters not being fubject to any regular plan of
refponfibility, were become dangerous rivals of
their mafter : their enemies knew how to infin-
uate fufpicions. The Conftable fell into difgrace
for having perfuaded the King to truft the promifes of Charles the Vth. and to grant him a free
paffage through France, as he went to chaftife
the rebellion of Ghent. The Emperor not keeping his engagements, the King and the court accufed the Conftable of having failed, either in
prudence or fidelity. He was obliged to leave
the court and return to private life, to conceal
himfelf from the purfuits of his enemies. The
Duke of Guife was alfo conftrained to quit the
court and give way to the ftorm, for having in-

curred

curred the difpleafure of the King, by caufing to be raifed upon the frontiers, without his confent, certain troops, which he fent to the Duke of Lorrain, his brother, at that time at war with the Anabaptifts.

The Conftable, and the Duke of Guife, thus difgraced, were replaced by two minifters of confummate experience, indefatigable induftry, and acknowledged abilities ; the Admiral D'Annebaut and the Cardinal de Tournon. The mediocrity of their fortune and extraction, excited little apprehenfion, that they would ever arrive, at that high power, of which the King had reafon to be jealous, and which he dreaded in the hands of his fubjects. This Prince, who underftood mankind, and was become unquiet and fufpicious fince his difgraces, had long refolved to difmifs from his perfon, the Conftable and the Duke, notwithftanding the long confidence with which he had honored them ; believing that he fhould not be able to govern, according to his own mind, while he fhould have about him two perfons, whofe credit and reputation were capable of balancing his will. He dreaded in the Conftable that profound experience, and that lively penetration, from which he could not conceal his moft hidden fecrets. Every thing was to him fufpicious in the Guifes. Their illuftrious birth, their reftlefs humor, their active genius, that ardent character to embrace every occafion to aggrandize themfelves, and that ambition capable of forming projects the moft vaft and daring. As the judicial courts had no independence, and there was no regular judicature for impeachments, there could be no rational refponfibility. The King could inflict none but arbitrary punifhments ; there was no tribunal, but the States

General

General and their committees, and among thefe the minifters had as many friends as the King.— The minifters therefore thought themfelves, and as the conftitution then ftood, they really were, fo nearly equal to the King in power, that they might do as they pleafed with impunity. They prefumed too far, and the King was juftly offended: but had no remedy, but in the affaffination or difmiffion of his minifters—he chofe the latter; though in the fequel we fhall fee many inftances, in fimilar cafes, of the former: In the laft years of his life, this monarch, if we may call by that name a Prince who was in effect, nothing more than the firft individual in a miferable oligarchy, fecretly recommended to Prince Henry his fon, to diftruft the exceffive power of his fubjects, and efpecially of the houfe of Guife, whofe elevation would infallibly difturb the repofe of the kingdom. Francis now faw and felt, that the houfe of Guife was become, as the houfe of Bourbon had been before, a dangerous rival of the houfe of Valois.

Ambition, difappointed and difgraced by a King, commonly becomes obfequious to the heir apparent, or oftenfible fucceffor. In 1547, Henry the fecond, the fucceffor of Francis the firft, difregarding the advice and example of his father, difmiffed from his court and fervice, the Admiral and Cardinal, though poffeffed of his fecrets of the ftate; and placed again at the head of affairs, the Conftable Anne of Montmorency, and Francis of Lorrain, fon of Claud Duke of Guife, who foon engaged the confidence of the young King, and regulated every thing at his court. Their authority was equal: But, as has been once obferved, nature has decreed, *that*

a perfect

a perfect equality shall never long exist between any two mortals. The views, the conduct and the characters of the two ministers, were unlike in all things. The Constable advanced in years, was naturally fond of peace: Formed by a long experience in the art of government, he enjoyed an high reputation for wisdom, and held the first place in the conduct of affairs of state. The Duke, in the flower of his age, captivated by an elevated genius and sprightly wit, united with a robust constitution and a noble figure, the affections of the King. Henry treated him, almost as his equal ; admitted him to his conversations, his pleasures, and those exercises of the body which were suitable to his age and inclination. His affection for the Constable, was rather veneration : His attachment to the Duke was familiarity. The conduct of the two favourites was very different ; the one an enemy of all show, urged with a certain severity, from which age is seldom exempted, the necessity of economy. He even opposed the profusion of the Prince. His austere virtue inspired a contempt for foreigners, and rendered him little solicitous for the affection of the French. The Duke of Guise, affable and popular, gained by his liberalities and politeness, the hearts of the people and the soldiers. With a generous warmth, he protected the unfortunate, and conciliated the esteem of strangers.

Inclinations and conduct so opposite, soon produced jealousies, between the two ministers, equally beloved of the King. To insinuate themselves further into the royal graces, and make themselves masters of his favors, they exerted all their skill, address and efforts. Their emulation
and

and ambition were ftimulated by their neareft relations, and private friends. The Conftable was irritated by his Nephew Gafpard de *Coligni*, Lord of Chatillon, who had fucceeded to the Admiral D'Annebaut, and who was not lefs diftinguifhed for his policy, than eminent for valor. The Duke of Guife was animated, by the Cardinal Charles of Lorrain, his brother, who united the fplendor of the Roman purple, to a noble figure, profound erudition and uncommon eloquence.

Hence forward the dæmon of rivalry, haunted the two houfes of Guife and Montmorency : and fortune did not fail to open a vaft career, to the animated emulation of the two competitors.

No. 4.

C'eft là le propre de l'efprit humain, que les exemples ne corrigent perfonne ; les fottifes des peres font perdues pour leurs enfans ; il faut que chaque generation faffe les fiennes.

LET us now attempt a performance of the promife at the clofe of our firft number : Men, in their primitive conditions, however favage, were undoubtedly gregarious—and they continue to be focial, not only in every ftage of civilization, but in every poffible fituation in which they can be placed. As nature intended them for fociety, fhe has furnifhed them with paffions, appetites, and propenfities, as well as a variety of faculties, calculated both for their individual enjoyment, and to render them ufeful to each other in their focial connections. There is none among them

D   more

more effential or remarkable, than the *paffon for diftinction*. A defire to be obferved, confidered, efteemed, praifed, beloved, and admired by his fellows, is one of the earlieft, as well as keeneft difpofitions difcovered in the heart of man. If any one fhould doubt the exiftence of this propenfity, let him go and attentively obferve the journeymen, and apprentices in the firft workfhop, or the oarfmen in a cockboat—a family or a neighbourhood—the inhabitants of a houfe, or the crew of a fhip—a fchool or a college—a city, or a village—a favage, or civilized people—an hofpital, or a church—the bar, or the exchange —a camp, or a court. Wherever men, women or children, are to be found, whether they be old or young—rich or poor—high or low—wife or foolifh—ignorant or learned—every individual is feen to be ftrongly actuated by a defire to be feen, heard, talked of, approved and refpected by the people about him, and within his knowledge.

Moral writers have, by immemorial ufage, a right to make a free ufe of the poets.

The love of praife, howe'er conceal'd by art,
Reigns more or lefs, and glows in every heart ;
The proud to gain it, toils on toils endure,
The modeft fhun it, but to make it fure.
O'er globes and fceptres, now on thrones it fwells,
Now, trims the midnight lamp in college cells.
'Tis tory, whig—it plots, prays, preaches, pleads,
Harrangues in Senates, fqueaks in mafquerades ;
It aids the dancer's heel, the writer's head,
And heaps the plain with mountains of the dead ;
Nor ends with life ; but nods in fable plumes
Adorns our herfe, and flatters on our tombs.

A regard to the fentiments of mankind concerning him, and to their difpofitions towards him, every man feels within himfelf ; and if he has reflected, and tried experiments, he has
found

found, that no exertion of his reafon—no effort of his will, can wholly diveft him of it. In proportion to our affection for the notice of others is our averfion to their neglect ; the ftronger the defire of the efteem of the public, the more powerful the averfion to their difapprobation—the more exalted the wifh for admiration, the more invincible the abhorrence of contempt. Every man not only defires the confideration of others, but he frequently compares himfelf with others, his friends or his enemies, and in proportion as he exults when he perceives that he has more of it, than they, he feels a keener affliction when he fees that one or more of them, are more refpected than himfelf.

This paffion, while it is fimply a defire to excel another, by fair induftry in the fearch of truth, and the practice of virtue, is properly called *Emulation*. When it aims at power, as a means of diftinction, it is *Ambition*. When it is in a fituation to fuggeft the fentiments of fear and apprehenfion, that another, who is now inferior, will become fuperior, it is denominated *Jealoufy*.— When it is in a ftate of mortification, at the fuperiority of another, and defires to bring him down to our level, or to deprefs him below us, it is properly called *Envy*. When it deceives a man into a belief of falfe profeffions of efteem or admiration, or into a falfe opinion of his importance in the judgment of the world, it is *Vanity*. Thefe obfervations alone would be fufficient to fhew, that this propenfity, in all its branches, is a principal fource of the virtues and vices, the happinefs and mifery of human life ; and that the hiftory of mankind is little more than a fimple narration of its operation and effects.

There

There is in human nature, it is true, fimple *Benevolence*—or an affection for the good of others—but, alone it is not a ballance for the felfifh affections. Nature then has kindly added to benevolence, the defire of reputation, in order to make us good members of fociety. *Spectemur agendo* expreffes the great principle of activity for the good of others. Nature has fanctioned the law of felf-prefervation by rewards and punifh-ments. The rewards of felfifh activity are life and health—the punifhments of negligence and indolence are want, difeafe and death. Each individual, it is true, fhould confider, that nature has enjoined the fame law on his neighbour, and therefore a refpect for the authority of nature would oblige him to refpect the rights of others as much as his own. But reafoning as abftrufe, though as fimple as this, would not occur to all men. The fame nature therefore has impofed another law, that of promoting the good, as well as refpecting the rights of mankind, and has fanctioned it by other rewards and punifhments. The rewards in this cafe, in this life, are *efteem* and *admiration* of others—the punifhments are *neglect* and *contempt*—nor may any one imagine that thefe are not as real as the others. The defire of the efteem of others is as real a want of nature as hunger—and the neglect and contempt of the world as fevere a pain, as the gout or ftone. It fooner and oftener produces defpair, and a detef-tation of exiftence—of equal importance to indi-viduals, to families, and to nations.—It is a prin-cipal end of government to regulate this paffion, which in its turn becomes a principal means of government. It is the only adequate inftrument of order and fubordination in fociety, and alone
commands

commands effectual obedience to laws, since without it neither human reason, nor standing armies, would ever produce that great effect. Every personal quality, and every blessing of fortune, is cherished in proportion to its capacity of gratifying this universal affection for the esteem, the sympathy, admiration and congratulations of the public. Beauty in the face, elegance of figure, grace of attitude and motion, riches, honors, every thing is weighed in the scale, and desired, not so much for the pleasure they afford, as the attention they command. As this is a point of great importance, it may be pardonable to expatiate a little, upon these particulars.

Why are the personal accomplishments of beauty, elegance and grace, held in such high estimation by mankind? Is it merely for the pleasure which is received from the sight of these attributes? By no means: The taste for such delicacies is not universal—in those who feel the most lively sense of them, it is but a slight sensation, and of shortest continuance; but those attractions command the notice and attention of the public —they draw the eyes of spectators: This is the charm that makes them irresistible. Is it for such fading perfections that an husband or a wife is chosen? Alas, it is well known, that a very short familiarity, totally destroys all sense and attention to such properties; and on the contrary, a very little time and habit destroys all the aversion to uglines and deformity, when unattended with disease or ill-temper: Yet beauty and address are courted and admired, very often, more than discretion, wit, sense, and many other accomplishments and virtues, of infinitely more importance to the happiness of private life, as

well

well as to the utility and ornament of fociety.
Is it for the momentous purpofe of dancing and
drawing, painting and mufic, riding or fencing,
that men and women are deftined in this life or
any other? Yet thofe who have the beft means
of education, beftow more attention and expenfe
on thofe, than on more folid acquifitions. Why?
Becaufe they attract more forcibly the attention
of the world, and procure a better advancement
in life. Notwithftanding all this, as foon as an
eftablifhment in life is made, they are found to
have anfwered their end, and are laid afide neglected.

Is there any thing in birth, however illuftrious or fplendid, which fhould make a difference
between one man and another? If, from a common anceftor, the whole human race is defcended, they are all of the fame family. How then
can they diftinguifh families into the more or the
lefs ancient? What advantage is there in an illuftration of an hundred or a thoufand years?
Of what avail are all thefe hiftories, pedigrees,
traditions? What foundation has the whole fcience of genealogy and heraldry? Are there differences in the breeds of men, as there are in
thofe of horfes? If there are not, thefe fciences
have no foundation in reafon—in prejudice they
have a very folid one: All that philofophy can
fay is, that there is a general prefumption, that
a man has had fome advantages of education, if
he is of a family of note. But this advantage
muft be derived from his father and mother
chiefly, if not wholly; of what importance is it
then, in this view, whether the family is twenty generations upon record, or only two?

The

The mighty fecret lies in this : An illuftrious defcent attracts the notice of mankind. A fingle drop of royal blood, however illegitimately fcattered, will make any man or woman proud or vain. Why ? Becaufe, although it excites the indignation of many, and the envy of more, it ftill attracts the *attention* of the world. Noble blood, whether the nobility be hereditary or elective, and indeed more in republican governments than in monarchies, leaft of all in defpotifms, is held in eftimation for the fame reafon. It is a name and a race that a nation has been interefted in, and is in the habit of refpecting.—Benevolence, fympathy, congratulation, have been fo long affociated to thofe names in the minds of the people, that they are become national habits. National gratitude defcends from the father to the fon, and is often ftronger to the latter than the former : It is often excited by remorfe, upon reflection on the ingratitude and injuftice with which the former has been treated. When the names of a certain family are read in all the gazettes, chronicles, records, and hiftories of a country for five hundred years, they become known, refpected, and delighted in by every body. A youth, a child of this extraction, and bearing this name, attracts the eyes and ears of all companies long before it is known or enquired, whether he be a wife man, or a fool. His name is often a greater diftinction, than a title, a ftar, or a garter. This it is which makes fo many men proud, and fo many others envious of illuftrious defcent. The pride is as irrational and contemptible as the pride of riches, and no more. A wife man will lament that any other diftinction than that of merit fhould be made. A good
man

man, will neither be proud nor vain of his birth ; but will earneftly improve every advantage he has for the public good. A cunning man will carefully conceal his pride ; but will indulge it in fecret, the more effectually, and improve his advantage to greater profit. But was any man ever known fo wife, or fo good, as really to def-pife birth or wealth ? Did you ever read of a man rifing to public notice, from obfcure begin-ings,who was not reflected on? Although with ev-ery liberal mind, it is an honor, and a proof of merit, yet it is a difgrace with mankind in gene-ral.—What a load of fordid obloquy and envy has every fuch man to carry ? The contempt that is thrown upon obfcurity of anceftry aug-ments the eagernefs for the ftupid adoration that is paid to its illuftration.

This defire of the confideration of our fellow-men, and their congratulations in our joys, is not lefs invincible, than the defire of their fym-pathy in our forrows. It is a determination of our nature that lies at the foundation of our whole moral fyftem in this world, and may be connect-ed effentially with our deftination in a future ftate. Why do men purfue riches ? What is the end of avarice ?—Thefe queftions may be anfwer-ed in our next.

No. 5.

O fureur de fe diftinguer, que ne pouvez vous point !

THE labour and anxiety, the enterprizes, and adventures, that are voluntarily undertaken in purfuit of gain, are out of all proportion to the
utility

utility, convenience or pleasure of riches. A competence to satisfy the wants of nature, food and cloaths, a shelter from the seasons, and the comforts of a family, may be had for very little. The daily toil of the million, and of millions of millions, is adequate to a complete supply of these necessities and conveniences. With such accommodations thus obtained, the appetite is keener, the digestion more easy and perfect, and repose is more refreshing, than among the most abundant superfluities and the rarest luxuries. For what reason then, are any mortals averse to the situation of the farmer, mechanic or labourer ?— Why do we tempt the seas, and encompass the globe? Why do any men affront heaven and earth, to accumulate wealth, which will forever be useless to them ? Why do we make an ostentatious display of riches ? Why should any man be proud of his purse, houses, lands, or gardens? or in better words, why should the rich man glory in his riches ? What connection can there be between wealth and pride ?

The answer to all these questions is, *because riches attract the attention, consideration and congratulations of mankind ;* it is not because the rich have really more of ease or pleasure than the poor. Riches force the opinion on a man that he is the object of the congratulations of others ; and he feels that they attract the complaisance of the public. His senses all inform him that his neighbors have a natural disposition to harmonize with all those pleasing emotions, and agreeable sensations, which the elegant accommodations around him are supposed to excite.

His imagination expands, and his heart dilates at these charming illusions : and his attachment to his

E

his poffeffions increafes, as faft as his defire to accumulate more : not for the purpofes of beneficence or utility, but from the defire of illuftration.

Why, on the other hand, fhould any man be a-
fhamed to make known his poverty? Why fhould
thofe who have been rich, or educated in the houfes of the rich, entertain fuch an averfion, or be
agitated with fuch terror, at the profpect of lofing their property ? Or of being reduced to live
at an humbler table ? In a meaner houfe ? To
walk inftead of riding ? Or to ride without their
accuftomed equipage or retinue ? Why do we
hear of madnefs, melancholy, and fuicides, upon
bankruptcy, lofs of fhips, or any other fudden fall
from opulence to indigence, or mediocrity ? Afk
your reafon, what difgrace there can be in poverty ? What moral fentiment of approbation,
praife or honor can there be in a palace ? What
difhonor in a cottage ? What glory in a coach,
what fhame in a waggon ? Is not the fenfe of
propriety, and fenfe of merit, as much connected
with an empty purfe, as a full one ? May not a
man be as eftimable, amiable and refpectable, attended by his faithful dog, as if preceded and
followed by a train of horfes and fervants ? All
thefe queftions may be very wife ; and the ftoical
philofophy has her anfwers ready. But if you afk
the fame queftions of nature, experience, and
mankind, the anfwers will be directly oppofite to
thofe of _Epictetus_, viz. that there is more refpec-
tability in the eyes of the greater part of mankind, in the gaudy trappings of wealth, than
there is in genius or learning, wifdom or virtue.

The poor man's confcience is clear ; yet he is
afhamed. His character is irreproachable, yet
he

he is neglected and defpifed. He feels himfelf
out of the fight of others, groping in the dark.
Mankind take no notice of him : he rambles
and wanders unheeded.   In the midft of a
croud, at church, in the market, at a play, at an
execution or coronation, he is in as much obfcurity, as he would be in a garret or a cellar. He
is not difapproved, cenfured or reproached : *he
is only not feen.*   This total inattention is to
him, mortifying, painful and cruel.   He fuffers
a mifery from this confideration, which is fhar-
pened by the confcioufnefs that others have no
fellow feeling with him in this diftrefs.   If you
follow thefe perfons,however,into their fcenes of
life, you will find that there is a kind of figure
which the meaneft of them all, endeavors to make;
a kind of little grandeur and refpect, which the
moft infignificant ftudy and labour to procure,
in the fmall circle of their acquaintances.   Not
only the pooreft mechanic, but the man who
lives upon common charity, nay the common
beggars in the ftreets ; and not only thofe who
may be all innocent, but even thofe who have
abandoned themfelves to common infamy as pi-
rates, highwaymen and common thieves, court
a fet of admirers, and plume themfelves on that
fuperiority, which they have, or fancy they have,
over fome others.   There muft be one indeed
who is the laft and loweft of the human fpecies.
But there is no rifk in afferting that there is no
one, who believes and will acknowledge himfelf
to be the man.   To be wholly overlooked and
to know it, are intolerable.   Inftances of this are
not uncommon.   When a wretch could no longer attract the notice of a man, woman or child,
he muft be refpectable in the eyes of his dog.—
" Who will love me then ?" was the pathetic re-
ply

ply of one, who ftarved himfelf to feed his maf-
tiff, to a charitable paffenger who advifed him to
kill or fell the animal. In this " *who will love me
then*," there is a key to the human heart—to the
hiftory of human life and manners—and to the rife
and fall of Empires. To feel ourfelves unheeded, chills the moft pleafing hope—damps the
moft fond defire—-checks the moft agreeable
wifh—difappoints the moft ardent expectations
of human nature.

Is there in fcience and letters, a reward for the
labor they require ? Scholars learn the dead languages of antiquity, as well as the living tongues
of modern nations. Thofe of the eaft as well
as the weft. They puzzle themfelves and
others with metaphyfics and mathematics. They
renounce their pleafures, neglect their exercifes,
and deftroy their health : For what ? Is curiofity fo ftrong ? Is the pleafure that accompanies
the purfuit and acquifition of knowledge fo exquifite ? If *Crufoe*, on his ifland, had the library
of *Alexandria*, and a certainty that he fhould never again fee the face of man, would he ever open
a volume ? Perhaps he might ; but it is very probable he would read but little. A fenfe of duty ;
a love of truth ; a defire to alleviate the anxieties of ignorance, may, no doubt, have an influence on fome minds. But the univerfal object
and idol of men of letters is *reputation*. It is the
notoriety, the *celebration*, which conftitutes the
charm, which is to compenfate the lofs of appetite and fleep, and fometimes of riches and honors.

The fame ardent defire of the *congratulations* of
others in our joys, is the great incentive to the
purfuit of honors. This might be exemplified in
the

the career of civil and political life. That we may not be too tedious, let us inftance in military glory.

Is it to be fuppofed that the regular ftanding armies of Europe, engage in the fervice, from pure motives of patriotifm ? Are their officers men of contemplation and devotion, who expect their reward in a future life ? Is it from a fenfe of moral, or religious duty, that they rifk their lives, and reconcile themfelves to wounds ? Inftances of all thefe kinds may be found. But if any one fuppofes that all, or the greater part of thefe heroes, are actuated by fuch principles, he will only prove that he is unacqainted with them. Can their pay be confidered as an adequate encouragement ? This, which is no more than a very fimple and moderate fubfiftence, would never be a temptation to renounce the chances of fortune in other purfuits, together with the pleafures of domeftic life, and fubmit to this moft difficult and dangerous employment. No, it is the confideration and the chances of laurels, which they acquire by the fervice.

The foldier compares himfelf with his fellows, and contends for promotion to be a Corporal : the Corporals vie with each other to be Sergeants: the Sergeants will mount breaches to be Enfigns : and thus every man in an army is conftantly afpiring to be fomething higher, as every citizen in the commonwealth is conftantly ftruggling for a better rank, that he may draw the obfervation of more eyes.

No. 6.

Such bribes the rapid Greek o'er Afia hurl'd ;
For fuch, the fteady Romans fhook the world.

IN a city or a village, little employments and trifling diftinctions are contended for with equal eagernefs, as honors and offices in commonwealths and kingdoms.

What is it that bewitches mankind to marks and figns ? A Ribbon ? A Garter ? A Star ? A golden Key ? A Marfhall's Staff ? Or a white hickory Stick ? Though there is in fuch frivolities, as thefe, neither profit nor pleafure, nor any thing amiable, eftimable or refpectable ; yet experience teaches us, in every country of the world, they attract the attention of mankind more than parts or learning, virtue or religion. They are therefore fought with ardor, very often, by men poffeffed in the moft eminent degree, of all the more folid advantages of birth and fortuue, merit and fervices, with the beft faculties of the head, and the moft engaging recommendations of the heart.

Fame has been divided into three fpecies : Glory, which attends the great actions of lawgivers and heroes, and the management of the great commands and firft offices of State : Reputation, which is cherifhed by every gentleman : and Credit, which is fupported by merchants and tradefmen. But even this divifion is incomplete, becaufe the defire and the object of it, though it may be confidered in various lights, and under different modifications, is not confined to gentlemen nor merchants, but is common to every human being.— There are no men, who are not ambitious of diftinguifhing themfelves, and growing confiderable

ble among thofe, with whom they converfe.— This ambition is natural to the human foul : and as when it receives a happy turn, it is the fource of private felicity and public profperity ; and when it errs, produces private uneafinefs and public calamities. It is the bufinefs and duty of private prudence, of private and public education, and of national policy, to direct it to right objects. For this purpofe it fhould be confidered, that to every man who is capable of a worthy conduct, the pleafure from the approbation of worthy men is exquifite and inexpreffible.

It is curious to confider the final caufes of things, when the phyfical are wholly unknown. The intellectual and moral qualities, are moft within our power, and undoubtedly the moft effential to our happinefs. The perfonal qualities of health, ftrength, and agility, are next in importance. Yet, the qualities of fortune, fuch as birth, riches, and honors, though a man has lefs reafon to efteem himfelf for thefe, than for thofe of his mind or body, are, every where acknowledged, to glitter with the brighteft luftre, in the eyes of the world.

As virtue is the only rational fource, and eternal foundation of honor, the wifdom of nations, in the titles they have eftablifhed as the marks of order and fubordination, has generally given an intimation, not of perfonal qualities, nor of the qualities of fortune ; but of fome particular virtues, more efpecially becoming men, in the high ftations they poffefs. Reverence is attributed to the Clergy—veneration to Magiftrates—honor to Senators—ferenity, clemency, or mildnefs of difpofition to Princes. The fovereign authority and fupreme executive, have commonly titles that

that defignate power as well as virtue—as Majefty to Kings—magnificent, moft honored, and
fovereign Lords, to the government of Geneva
—noble mightineffes to the States of Friefland
—noble and mighty Lords to the States of Guel-
derland—noble great and venerable Lords to the
regency of Leyden—noble and grand mightineffes to the States of Holland—noble great and
venerable Lords, the regency of Amfterdam—noble mightineffes, the States of Utrecht—and high
mightineffes the States General.

A death bed, it is faid, fhews the emptinefs of
titles. That may be. But does it not equally
fhew the futility of richefs, power, liberty, and all
earthly things ? The cloud-capt towers, the gor-
geous palaces, the folemn temples, the great globe
itfelf, appear the bafelefs fabric of a vifion, and
life itfelf a tale, told by an ideot, full of found
and fury, fignifying nothing. Shall it be infer-
red from this, that fame, liberty, property and
life, fhall be always defpifed and neglected ? Shall
laws and government, which regulate fublunary
things be neglected, becaufe they appear baubles
at the hour of death ?

The wifdom and virtue of all nations have endeavored to regulate the paffion for refpect and
diftinction, and to reduce it to fome order in fociety, by titles marking the gradations of magif-
tracy, to prevent, as far as human power and policy can prevent, collifions among the paffions of
many purfuing the fame objects, and the rivalries, animofities, envy, jealoufy and vengeance,
which always refult from them.

Has there ever been a nation, who underftood
the human heart, better than the Romans ? Or
made a better ufe of the paffion for confideration,

tion, congratulation and diftinction ? They confidered, that as reafon is the guide of life, the
fenfes, the imagination and the affections are the
fprings of activity. Reafon holds the helm, but
paffions are the gales : and as the direct road
to thefe is through the fenfes, the language of
figns was employed by Roman wifdom to excite the emulation and active virtue of the citizens. *Diftinctions* of *conditions*, as well as of ages,
were made by difference of cloathing. The Lat-
iclave, or large flowing Robe, ftudded with
broad fpots of purple, the ancient diftinction of
their Kings, was, after the eftablifhment of the
Confulate, worn by the Senators, through the
whole period of the Republic and the Empire.—
The Tribunes of the people, were, after their inftitution, admitted to wear the fame venerable
fignal of fanctity and authority. The Angufti-
clave, or the fmaller robe, with narrower ftuds
of purple, was the diftinguifhing habit of Roman
Knights. The golden Ring was alfo peculiar to
Senators and Knights, and was not permitted to
be worn by any other citizens. The Prætext, or
long white Robe reaching down to the ancles,
bordered with purple, which was worn by the
principal Magiftrates, fuch as Confuls, Prætors,
Cenfors and fometimes on folemn feftivals, by
Senators. The chairs of ivory ; the lictors ;
the rods ; the axes ; the crowns of gold ; of i-
vory ; of flours ; of herbs ; of laurel branches ;
and of oak-leaves ; the civil and the mural
crowns ; their ovations; and their triumphs ;
every thing in religion, government and common life, among the Romans, was parade, reprefentation and ceremony. Every thing was ad-
dreffed to the emulation of the citizens, and ev-

ery thing was calculated to attract the attention, to allure the confideration, and excite the congratulations of the people ; to attach their hearts to individual citizens according to their merit ; and to their lawgivers, magiftrates, and judges, according to their ranks, ftations and importance in the State. And this was in the true fpirit of republics, in which form of government there is no other confiftent method of preferving order, or procuring fubmiffion to the laws. To fuch means as thefe, or to force, and a ftanding army, recourfe muft be had, for the guardianfhip of laws, and the protection of the people. It is univerfally true, that in all the Republics now remaining in Europe, there is, as there ever has been, a more conftant and anxious attention to fuch forms and marks of diftinctions, than there is in the Monarchies.

The policy of Rome was exhibited in its higheft perfection, in the triumph of Paulus Emillius over Perfeus. It was a ftriking exemplification of congratulation and fympathy, contrafted with each other. Congratulation with the conqueror : fympathy with the captive : both fuddenly changed into fympathy with the conqueror.—The defcription* of this triumph, is written with a pomp of language correfpondent to its dazzling magnificence. The reprefentation of the King, and his children, muft excite the pity of every reader who is not animated with the ferocious fentiments of Roman infolence and pride. Never was there a more moving leffon of the melancholy lot of humanity, than the contrafted fortunes of the Macedonian and the Roman.—The one divefted of his crown and throne, led in chains, with his children before his chariot

the

* Livy.

the other, blazing in gold and purple, to the capitol.   This inftructive leffon is given us by the
victor himfelf, in a fpeech to the people.   " My
" triumph, Romans, as if it had been in derifion
" of all human felicity, has been interpofed be-
" tween the funerals of my children, and both
" have been exhibited, as fpectacles, before you.
" Perfeus, who, himfelf a captive, faw his chil-
" dren led with him in captivity, now enjoys
" them in fafety.   I, who triumphed over him,
" having afcended the capitol, from the funeral
" chariot of one of my fons, defcended from
" that capitol, to fee another expire.   In the
" houfe of Paulus none remains but himfelf. But
" your felicity, Romans, and the profperous for-
" tune of the public, is a confolation to me under
" this deftruction of my family."
It is eafy to fee how fuch a fcene muft operate
on the hearts of a nation : how it muft affect the
paffion for diftinction : and how it muft excite
the ardor and virtuous emulation of the citizens.

No. 7,

The Senate's thanks, the Gazette's pompous tale,
With force refiftlefs, o'er the brave prevail.
This power has praife, that Virtue fcarce can warm,
Till fame fupplies the univerfal charm.

THE refult of the preceeding difcourfes is,
that avarice and ambition, vanity and pride,
jealoufy and envy, hatred and revenge, as well
as the love of knowledge and defire of fame are
very

very often nothing more than various modifications of that defire of the attention, confideration and congratulations of our fellow men,
which is the great fpring of focial activity ; that
all men compare themfelves with others, efpecially thofe with whom they moft frequently
converfe ; thofe, who, by their employments or
amufements, profeffions or offices, prefent themfelves moft frequently, at the fame time to the
view and thoughts of that public, little or great,
to which every man is known, that emulations
and rivalries naturally, and neceffarily are excited
by fuch comparifons ; that the moft heroic actions in war, the fublimeft virtues in peace, and
the moft ufeful induftry in agriculture, arts, manufactures and commerce, proceed from fuch emulations, on the one hand, and jealoufies, envy,
enmity, hatred, revenge, quarrels, factions, feditions and wars, on the other. The final caufe of
this conftitution of things is eafy to difcover.—
Nature has ordained it, as a conftant incentive to
activity and induftry, that, to acquire the attention and complacency, the approbation and admiration of their fellows, men might be urged to
conftant exertions of beneficence. By this deftination of their natures, men of all forts, even
thofe who have the leaft of reafon, virtue or benevolence, are chained down to an inceffant fervi-
tude to their fellow-creatures, labouring without
intermiffion to produce fomething which fhall
contribute to the comfort, convenience, pleafure,
profit or utility of fome or other of the fpecies ;
they are really thus conftituted by their own
vanity, flaves to mankind. Slaves, I fay again :
for what a folly is it ? On a felfifh fyftem, what
are the thoughts, paffions and fentiments of mankind

kind to us ? What is fame ? A fancied life, in
others breath. What is it to us, what fhall be
faid of us, after we are dead ? Or in Afia, Africa, or Europe, while we live ? There is no greater poffible or imaginable delufion : yet the im-
pulfe is irrefiftable. The language of nature to
man in his conftitution is this, " I have given
" you reafon, confcience, and benevolence : and
" thereby made you accountable for your actions,
" and capable of virtue, in which you will find
" your higheft felicity. But I have not confid-
" ed wholly in your laudable improvement of
" thefe divine gifts. To them I have fuperad-
" ded a paffion in your bofoms, for the notice
" and regard of your fellow mortals, which, if
" you perverfely violate your duty, and wholly
" neglect the part affigned you, in the fyftem of
" the world, and the fociety of mankind, fhall
" torture you, from the cradle to the grave."

Nature has taken effectual care of her own
work. She has wrought the paffions into the
texture and effence of the foul—and has not left
it in the power of art to deftroy them. To regulate and not to eradicate them is the province
of policy. It is of the higheft importance to education, to life and to fociety, not only that they
fhould not be deftroyed, but that they fhould be
gratified, encouraged, and arranged on the fide
of virtue. To confine our obfervations at prefent to that great leading paffion of the foul,
which has been fo long under our confideration :
What difcouragement, diftrefs and defpair, have
not been occafioned by its difappointment ? To
confider one inftance, among many, which happen continually in fchools and colleges. Put a
fuppofition of a pair of twin brothers, who have
been

been nourifhed by the fame nurfe, equally encouraged by their parents and preceptors, with
equal genius, health and ftrength, purfuing their
ftudies with equal ardor and fuccefs. One, is at
length overtaken by fome ficknefs, and in a few
days the other, who efcapes the influenza, is advanced fome pages before him. This alone will
make the ftudies of the unfortunate child, when
he recovers his health, difguftful. As foon as he
lofes the animating hope of pre-eminence, and is
conftrained to acknowledge, a few others of his
fourm or clafs, his fuperiors, he becomes incapable of induftrious application. Even the fear of
the ferule or the rod, will after this be ineffectual. The terror of punifhment, by forcing attention, may compel a child to perform a tafk—
but can never infufe that ardor for ftudy, which
alone can arrive at great attainments. Emulation really feems to produce genius, and the defire of fuperiority to create talents. Either this,
or the reverfe of it, muft be true; and genius
produces emulation, and natural talents, the defire of fuperiority—for they are always found
together, and what God and nature have united,
let no audacious legiflator prefume to put afun-
der. When the love of glory inkindles in the
heart, and influences the whole foul, then, and
only then, may we depend on a rapid progreffion
of the intellectual faculties. The awful feeling
of a mortified emulation, is not peculiar to children. In an army, or a navy, fometimes the intereft of the fervice requires, and oftener perhaps
private intereft and partial favor prevail, to promote officers over their fuperiors, or feniors.—
But the confequence is, that thofe officers can
never ferve again together. They muft be dif-
                                        tributed

tributed in different corps, or fent on different commands. Nor is this the worft effect : It almoft univerfally happens, that the fuperceded officer feels his heart broken by his difgrace.— His mind is enfeebled by grief, or difturbed by refentment—and the inftances have been very rare, of any brilliant action performed by fuch an officer. What a monument to this character of human nature is the long lift of yellow Admirals in the Britifh fervice !—Confider the effects of fimilar difappointments in civil affairs. Minifters of State, are frequently difplaced in all countries—and what is the confequence ? Are they feen happy in a calm refignation to their fate ? Do they turn their thoughts from their former employments, to private ftudies or bufinefs ? Are they men of pleafant humour, and engaging converfation ? Are their hearts at eafe? Or is their converfation a conftant effufion of complaints and murmurs, and their breaft the refidence of refentment and indignation, of grief and forrow, of malice and revenge ? Is it common to fee a man get the better of his ambition, and defpife the honors he once poffeffed ; or is he commonly employed in projects upon projects, intrigues after intrigues, and manœuvers on manœuvers to recover them ? So fweet and delightful to the human heart is that complacency and admiration, which attends public offices, whether they are conferred by the favor of a Prince, derived from hereditary defcent, or obtained by election of the people, that a mind muft be funk below the feelings of humanity, or exalted by religion or philofophy far above the common character of men, to be infenfible, or to conquer its fenfibility. Pretenfions to fuch con-

queſts

quefts are not uncommon ; but the fincerity of
fuch pretenders is often rendered fufpicious, by
their conftant converfation and conduct, and e-
ven by their countenances. The people are fo
fenfible of this, that a man in this predicament is
always on the compaffionate lift, and, except in
cafes of great refentment againft him for fome
very unpopular principles or behavior, they are
found to be always ftudying fome other office
for a difappointed man, to confole him in his affliction. In fhort, the theory of Education, and
the fcience of government, may be reduced to
the fame fimple principle, and be all comprehended in the knowledge of the means of activity,
conducting, controling and regulating the emulation and ambition of the citizens.

No. 8.

This mournful truth is every where confefs'd,
Slow rifes Worth by Poverty deprefs'd.

IF we attempt to analyze our ideas ftill further, upon this fubject, we fhall find, that the
expreffions we have hitherto ufed, *attention, confideration* and *congratulation*, comprehend with
fufficient accuracy, the general object of the paffion for diftinction, in the greater part of mankind. There are not a few, from him who burned a temple, to the multitudes who plunge into
low debauchery, who deliberately feek it by
crimes and vices. The greater number, however, fearch for it, neither by vices nor virtues :
But by the means, which common fenfe and every

ery day's experience fhows, are moft fure to obtain it ; by riches, by family records, by play,
and other frivolous perfonal accomplifhments.—
But there are a few, and God knows but a few,
who aim at fomething more : They aim at approbation as well as attention ; at efteem as well
as confideration ; and at admiration and gratitude, as well as congratulation. Admiration is
indeed the complete idea of approbation, congratulation,and wonder united. This laft defcription
of perfons is the tribe out of which proceeds
your patriots and heroes, and moft of the great
benefactors to mankind. But for our humiliation, we muft ftill remember, that even in thefe
efteemed, beloved and adored characters, the
paffion, although refined by the pureft moral fentiments, and intended to be governed by the beft
principles, is a paffion ftill ; and therefore, like
all other human defires, unlimited and infatiable.
No man was ever contented with any given
fhare of this human adoration. When Cæfar declared that he had lived enough to glory ; Cæfar
might deceive himfelf, but he did not deceive
the world, who faw his declaration contradicted
by every action of his fubfequent life. Man conftantly craves for more, even when he has no
rival : But when he fees another poffeffed of
more, or drawing away from himfelf a part of
what he had, he feels a mortification, arifing
from the lofs of a good he thought his own :—
His defire is difappointed : The pain of a want
unfatisfied, is increafed by a refentment of an injuftice, as he thinks it : He accufes his rival of a
theft or robbery, and the public of taking away,
what was his property, and giving it to another.
Thefe feelings and refentments, are but other

G   names

names for jealoufy and envy ; and altogether,
they produce fome of the keeneft and moft tor-
menting of all fentiments. Thefe fermentations
of the paflions are fo common and fo well known,
that the people generally prefume, that a perfon
in fuch circumftancces, is deprived of his judgment, if not of his veracity and reafon. It is too
generally a fufficient anfwer to any complaint,
to any fact alledged, or argument advanced, to
fay that it comes from a difappointed man.

There is a voice within us, which feems to intimate, that real merit fhould govern the world ;
and that men ought to be refpected only in
proportion to their talents, virtues and fervices.
But the queftion always has been, how can this
arrangement be accomplifhed ? How fhall the
men of merit be difcovered ? How fhall the pro-
portions of merit be afcertained and graduated ?
Who fhall be the judge ? When the government
of a great nation is in queftion, fhall the whole
nation choofe ? Will fuch a choice be better
than chance ? Shall the whole nation vote for
Senators ? Thirty millions of votes, for example, for each Senator in France ! It is obvious
that this would be a lottery of millions of blanks
to one prize, and that the chance of having wifdom and integrity in a Senator by hereditary
defcent would be far better.   There is no individual perfonally known to an hundredth part
of the nation.   The voters then muft be expofed
to deception, from intrigues and manœuvres,
without number, that is to fay, from all the chicanery, impoftures and falfhoods imaginable,
with fcarce a poffibility of prefering real merit.
Will you divide the nation into diftricts, and let
each diftrict choofe a Senator ? This is giving up
the

the idea of national merit, and annexing the honor and the truſt to an accident, that of living on
a particular ſpot An hundred or a thouſand men
of the firſt merit in a nation, may live in one city,
and none at all of this deſcription in ſeveral whole
provinces. Real merit is ſo remote from the
knowledge of whole nations, that were magiſtrates to be choſen by that criterion alone, and
by an univerſal ſuffrage, diſſentions and venality
would be endleſs. The difficulties ariſing from
this ſource, are ſo obvious and univerſal, that nations have tried all ſorts of experiments to avoid
them.

As no appetite in human nature is more univerſal than that for honor, and real merit is confined to a very few, the numbers who thirſt for
reſpect, are out of all proportion to thoſe who
ſeek it only by merit. The great majority trouble themſelves little about merit, but apply themſelves to ſeek for honor, by which means they ſee
will more eaſily and certainly obtain it, by diſplay-
ing their taſte and addreſs, their wealth and magnificence, their ancient parchments, pictures, and
ſtatues, and the virtues of their anceſtors ; and if
theſe fail, as they ſeldom have done, they have
recourſe to artifice, diſſimulation, hypocriſy, flat-
tery, impoſture, empiriciſm, quackery and bribe-
ry. What chance has humble, modeſt, obſcure
and poor merit, in ſuch a ſcramble ? Nations, perceiving that the ſtill ſmall voice of merit, was
drowned in the inſolent roar of ſuch dupes of
impudence and knavery, in national elections,
without a poſſibility of a remedy, have fought for
ſomething more permanent than the popular
voice to deſignate honor. Many nations have
attempted to annex it to land, preſuming that a
                                              good

good eftate would at leaft furnifh means of a good
education ; and have refolved that thofe who
fhould poffefs certain territories, fhould have certain legiflative, executive and judicial powers, o-
ver the people. Other nations have endeavoured to connect honor with offices ; and the names
and ideas at leaft of certain moral virtues and intellectual qualities have been by law annexed to
certain offices, as veneration, grace, excellence,
honor, ferenity, majefty. Other nations have attempted to annex honor to families, without regard to lands or offices. The Romans allowed
none, but thofe who had poffeffed curule offices,
to have ftatues or portraits. He, who had images or pictures of his anceftors, was called noble.
He who had no ftatue or pictures but his own,
was called a new man. Thofe who had none at
all, were ignoble. Other nations have united all
thofe inftitutions ; connected lands, offices and
families—made them all defcend together, and
honor, public attention, confideration and congratulation, along with them. This has been the
policy of Europe ; and it is to this inftitution
which fhe owes her fuperiority in war and peace,
in legiflation and commerce, in agriculture, navigation, arts, fciences and manufactures, to Afia
and Africa. Thefe families, thus diftinguifhed
by property, honors and privileges, by defending themfelves, have been obliged to defend the
people againft the encroachments of defpotifm.
They have been a civil and political militia, conftantly watching the defigns of the ftanding armies, and courts ; and by defending their own
rights, liberties, properties, and privileges, they
have been obliged, in fome degree, to defend
thofe of the people, by making a common caufe
with

with them. But there were feveral effential
tial defects in this policy : one was that the people took no rational meafures to defend themfelves, either againft thefe great families, or the
courts. They had no adequate reprefentation of
themfelves in the fovereignty. Another was that
it never was determined where the fovereignty
refided—generally it was claimed by Kings ; but
not admitted by the nobles. Sometimes every
Baron pretended to be fovereign in his own ter-
ritory ; at other times the fovereignty was claimed by an affembly of nobles, under the name
of States or Cortes. Sometimes the United authority of the King and States was called the fovereignty. The common people had no adequate and
independent fhare in the legiflatures, and found
themfelves harraffed to difcover who was the fovereign, and whom they ought to obey, as much
as they ever had been or could be to determine
who had the moft merit. A thoufand years of Barons' wars, caufing univerfal darknefs, ignorance
and barbarity, ended at laft in fimple monarchy, not
by exprefs ftipulation, but by tacit acquiefcence,
in almoft all Europe ; the people prefering a certain fovereignty in a fingle perfon, to endlefs difputes, about merit and fovereignty, which never
did and never will produce any thing but ariftocratical anarchy ; and the nobles contenting themfelves with a fecurity of their property and privileges, by a government of fixed laws, regiftered and
interpreted by a judicial power, which they called fovereign tribunals, though the legiflation
and execution were in a fingle perfon. In this
fyftem to controul the nobles, the church joined
the Kings and common people.

The progrefs of reafon, letters and fcience, has
weakened

weakened the church and ftrengthened the common people ; who, if they are honeftly and prudently conducted by thofe who have their confidence, will moft infallibly obtain a fhare in every legiflature. But if the common people are advifed to aim at collecting the whole fovereignty in fingle national affemblies, as they are by the Duke de la *Rochefoucault* and the Marquis of *Condercet ;* or at the abolition of the Regal executive authority ; or at a divfion of the executive power, as they are by a pofthumous publication of the Abby de *Mably,** they will fail of their defired liberty, as certainly as emulation and rivalry are founded in human nature, and infeparable from civil affairs. It is not to flatter the paffions of the people, to be fure, nor is it the way to obtain a prefent enthufiaftic popularity, to tell them that in a fingle affembly, they will act as arbitrarily and tyranically as any defpot, but it is a facred truth, and as demonftrable as any propofition whatever, that a fovereignty in a fingle affembly muft neceffarily, and will certainly be exercifed by a majority, as tyrannically as any fovereignty was ever exercifed by Kings or Nobles. And if a ballance of paffions and interefts is not fcientifically concerted, the prefent ftruggle in Europe will be little beneficial to mankind, and produce nothing but another thoufand years of feudal fanaticifm, under new and ftrange names.

* The Abby's Project has fince been tried in a quintuple Directory.

———

Tis from high life, high characters are drawn,
A Saint in *crape*, is twice a Saint in *lawn*.

PROVIDENCE, which has placed one thing over against another, in the moral as well as physical world, has surprisingly accommodated the qualities of men, to answer one another. There is a remarkable disposition in mankind to congratulate with others in their joys and prosperity, more than to sympathise with them in their sorrows and adversity. We may appeal to experience. There is less disposition to congratulation with genius, talents, or virtue, than there is with beauty, strength and elegance of person; and less with these than with the gifts of fortune and birth, wealth and fame. The homage of the world is devoted to these last, in a remarkable manner. Experience concurs with religion in pronouncing, most decisively, that this world is not the region of virtue or happiness; both are here at school, and their struggles with ambition, avarice, and the desire of fame, appear to be their discipline and exercise. The gifts of fortune are more level to the capacities, and more obvious to the notice of mankind in general; and congratulation with the happiness, or fancied happiness of others, is agreeable; sympathy with their misery is disagreeable: from the former sources we derive pleasure, from the latter pain. The sorrow of the company at a funeral, may be more profitable to moral purposes, by suggesting useful reflections, than the mirth at a wedding; but it is not so vivid, nor so sincere. The acclamations of
the

the populace, at an ovation or triumph, at a coronation, or inftallation, are from the heart, and their joy is unfeigned. Their grief at a public execution is lefs violent at leaft : if their feelinge at fuch fpectacles were very diftreffing. they would be lefs eager to attend them. What is the motive of that ardent curiofity to fee fights and fhews of exultation—the proceffions of Princes—the oftentation of wealth—the magnificence of equipage, retinue, furniture, buildings, and entertainment ? There is no other anfwer to be given to thefe queftions, than the gaiety of heart, the joyous feelings of congratulation with fuch appearances of felicity. And for the vindication of the ways of God to man, and the perpetual confolation of the many, who are fpectators, it is certainly true, that their pleafure is always as great, aud commonly much greater, than that of the few who are the actors.

National paffions and habits are unweildy, unmanageable and formidable things. The number of perfons in any country, who are known even by name or reputation, to all the inhabitants, is, and ever muft be, very fmall. Thofe, whofe characters have attracted the affections, as well as the attention of an whole people, acquire an influence and afcendancy that it is difficult to refift. In proportion as men rife higher in the world, whether by election, defcent or appointment, and are expofed to the obfervation of greater numbers of people, the effects of their own paffions, and of the affections of others for them become more ferious, interefting and dangerous. In elective governments, where firft magiftrates and fenators are at ftated intervals to be chofen, thefe, if there are no parties, become

at

at every frefh election, more known, confidered and beloved, by the whole nation. But if the nation is divided into two parties, thofe who vote for a man, become the more attached to him for the oppofition, that is made by his enemies This national attachment to an elective firft magiftrate, where there is no competition, is very great : but where there is a competition, the paffions of his party, are inflamed by it, into a more ardent enthufiafm. If there are two candidates, each at the head of a party, the nation becomes divided into two nations, each of which is, in fact, a moral perfon, as much as any community can be fo, and are foon, bitterly enraged againft each other.

It has been already faid, that in proportion as men rife higher in the world, and are expofed to the obfervation of greater numbers, the effects of thefe paffions are more ferious and alarming. Impreffions on the feelings of the individual, are deeper ; and larger portions of mankind become interefted in them. When you rife to the firft ranks, and confider the firft men ; a nobility who are known and refpected at leaft, perhaps habitually efteemed and beloved by a nation ; Princes and Kings, on whom the eyes of all men are fixed, and whofe every motion is regarded, the confequences of wounding their feelings are dreadful, becaufe the feelings of an whole nation, and fometimes of many nations, are wounded at the fame time. If the fmalleft variation is made in their fituation, relatively to each other ; if one who was inferior is raifed to be fuperior, unlefs it be by fixed laws, whofe evident policy and neceffity may take away difgrace, nothing but war, carnage and vengeance has ever been the ufual con-

M   fequence

fequence of it. In the examples of the houfes *Valois* and *Bourbon*, *Guife* and *Montmorency*, *Guife* and *Bourbon*, and *Guife* and *Valois*, we have already feen very grave effects of thefe feelings, and the hiftory of an hundred years, which followed, is nothing but a detail of other, and more tragical effects of fimilar caufes.

To any one who has never confidered the force of *national attention, confideration, and congratulation*, and the caufes, natural and artificial, by which they have been excited, it will be curious to read, in *Plato*'s Alcibiades, the manner in which thefe national attachments to their kings, were created by the ancient Perfians. The policy of the modern monarchies of Europe, feems to be an exact imitation of that of the Perfian Court, as it is explained by the Grecian philofopher. In France, for example, the pregnancy of the Queen is announced with great folemnity to the whole nation. Her Majefty is fcarcely afflicted with a pain which is not formally communicated to the public. To this embryo the minds of the whole nation are turned ; and they follow him, day by day, in their thoughts, till he is born. The whole people have a right to be prefent at his birth ; and as many as the Chamber will hold, crowd in, till the Queen and Prince are almoft fuffocated with the loyal curiofity and affectionate folicitude of their fubjects. In the cradle, the principal perfonages of the kingdom, as well as all the Ambaffadors, are from time to time prefented to the royal infant. To thoufands who prefs to fee him, he is daily fhewn from the nurfery. Of every ftep in his education ; and of every gradation of his youthful growth, in body and mind, the public is informed in the Gazettes. Not a ftroke

of

of wit, not a sprightly sally, not a trait of gener
ous affection, can escape him, but the world is
told of it, and very often pretty fictions are contrived, for the same purpose, where the truth
will not furnish materials. Thus it becomes the
national fashion, it is the *tone* of the city and the
court, to think and converse daily about the dauphin. When he accedes to the throne, the same
attention is continued, till he dies.

In elective governments, something very like
this, always takes place, towards the first character: his person, countenance, character and actions, are made the daily contemplation and con-
versation of the whole people. Hence arises the
danger of a division of this attention —where
there are rivals for the first place, the national
attention and passions are divided, and thwart
each other—the collision enkindles fires—the con-
flicting passions interest all ranks — they produce
slanders and libels first, mobs and seditions next,
and civil war, with all her hissing snakes, burning torches, and haggard horrors at last.

This is the true reason, why all civilized free
nations have found, by experience, the necessity of
separating, from the body of the people, and ev-
en from the legislature, the distribution of honors, and confering it on the executive authority
of government. When the emulation of all the
citizens looks up to one point, like the rays of
a circle from all parts of the circumference, meet-
ing and uniting in the centre, you may hope for
uniformity, consistency and subordination: but
when they look up to different individuals, or
assemblies, or councils, you may expect all the
deformities, eccentricities, and confusion, of the
Polemick system.

No.

No. 10.

———

" Wife if a Minifter, but if a King,
" More wife, more learn'd, more juft, more every thing.

THERE is fcarcely any truth more certain, or more evident, than that the nobleffe of Europe, are, in general lefs happy than the common people. There is one irrefragible proof of it, which is, that they do not maintain their own population. Families, like ftars, or candles, which you will, are going out continually; and without frefh recruits from the plebeians, the nobility would in time be extinct. If you make allowances for the ftate, which they are condemned by them, felves, and the world, to fupport, they are poorer than the poor—deeply in debt—and tributary to ufurious capitalifts, as greedy as the Jews.— The kings of Europe, in the fight of a philofopher, are the greateft flaves on earth, how often foever we may call them defpots, tyrants, and other rude names, in which our pride and vanity takes a wonderful delight : they have the leaft exercife of their inclinations, the leaft perfonal liberty, and the leaft free indulgence of their paffions, of any men alive. Yet how rare are the inftances of refignations, and how univerfal is the ambition to be noble, and the wifh to be royal.

Experience and philofophy are loft upon mankind. The attention of the world has a charm in it, which few minds can withftand. The people confider the condition of the great in all thofe delufive colours, in which imagination can paint and gild it, and reafon can make little refiftance, to this impetuous propenfity. To better their
condition

condition, to advance their fortunes, without limits, is the object of their conftant defire, the
employment of all their thoughts by day and by
night. They feel a peculiar fympathy with that
pleafure, which they prefume thofe enjoy, who
are already powerful, celebrated and rich. " We
favour (fays a great writer) all their inclinations,
and forward all their wifhes. What pity, we
think, that any thing fhould fpoil and corrupt fo
agreeable a fituation : we could even wifh them
immortal ; and it feems hard to us, that death
fhould at laft put an end to fuch perfect enjoyment. It is cruel, we think in nature, to compel them from their exalted flations, to that humble, but hofpitable home, which fhe has provided
for all her children. Great King, live forever !
is the compliment, which, after the manner of
Eaftern adulation, we fhould readily make them,
if experience did not teach us its abfurdity.—
Every calamity that befalls them, every injury
that is done them, excites in the breaft of the
fpectator, ten times more compaffion and refentment, than he would have felt, had the fame
things happened to other men. It is the misfortune of Kings only, which afford the proper fubjects for tragedy ; they refemble, in this refpect,
the misfortune of lovers. Thefe two fituations
are the chief which intereft us on the ftage ; becaufe, in fpight of all that reafon and experience
can tell us to the contrary, the prejudices of the
imagination, attach to thefe two ftates. a happinefs fuperior to any other. To difturb or put an
end to fuch perfect enjoyment, feems to be the
moft atrocious of all injuries. The traitor, who
confpires againft the life of his monarch, is tho't
a greater monfter, than any other murderer. All
the

the innocent blood that was fhed in the civil wars, provoked lefs indignation than the death of Charles Ift. A ftranger to human nature, who faw the indifference of men about the mifery of their inferiors, and the regret and indignation which they feel for the misfortunes and fufferings of thofe above them, would be apt to imagine, that pain muft be more agonizing, and the convulfions of death more terrible to perfons of higher rank, than to thofe of meaner ftations.

" Upon this difpofition of mankind, to go along with all the paffions of the rich and powerful, is founded the diftinction of ranks, and the order of fociety. Our obfequioufnefs to our fuperiors more frequently arifes from our admiration for the advantages of their fituation, than from any private expectations of benefit from their good will. Their benefits can extend but to a few ; but their fortunes intereft almoft every body. We are eager to affift them in compleating a fyftem of happinefs that approaches fo near to perfection ; and we defire to ferve them for their own fake, without any other recompence but the vanity or the honor of obliging them. Neither is our deference to their inclinations founded chiefly, or altogether, upon a regard to the utility of fuch fubmiffion, and to the order of fociety, which is beft fupported by it. Even when the order of fociety feems to require that we fhould oppofe them, we can hardly bring ourfelves to do it. That kings are the fervants of the people, to be obeyed, refifted, depofed, or punifhed, as the public conveniency may require, is the doctrine of reafon and philofophy ; but it is not the doctrine of nature. Nature would teach us to fubmit to them, for their

their own fakes, to tremble and bow down before their exalted ftation, to regard their fmile
as a reward fufficient to compenfate any fervices,
and to dread their difpleafure, though no other
evil was to follow from it, as the fevereft of all
mortifications. To treat them in any refpect as
men, to reafon and difpute with them upon ordinary occafions, requires fuch refolution, that
there are few men whofe magnanimity can fupport them in it, unlefs they are likewife affifted
by familiarity and acquaintance. The ftrongeft
motives, the moft furious paffions, fear, hatred
and refentment, are fcarce fufficient to balance
this natural difpofition to refpect them : and
their conduct muft either juftly or unjuftly, have
excited the higheft degree of all thofe paffions,
before the bulk of the people can be brought to
oppofe them with violence, or to defire to fee
them either punifhed or depofed. Even when
the people have been brought to this length, they
are apt to relent every moment, and eafily re-
lapfe into their habitual ftate of deference. They
cannot ftand the mortification of their monarch ;
compaffion foon takes the place of refentment,
they forget all paft provocations, their old principles of loyalty revive, and they run to re-eftablifh the ruined authority of their old mafters,
with the fame violence with which they had
oppofed it. The death of Charles the firft,
brought about the reftoration of the royal family. Compaffion for James the fecond, when he
was feized by the populace, in making his efcape on fhip board, had almoft prevented the
revolution, and made it go on more heavily than
before.

" Do the great feem infenfible of the eafy
price

price, as which they may acquire the public admiration ; or do they feem to imagine, that to them, as to other men, it muft be the purchafe either of fweat or of blood ? By what important accomplifhments is the young nobleman inftructed to fupport the dignity of his rank, and to render himfelf worthy of that fuperiority over his fellow citizens, to which the virtue of his anceftors had raifed them ? Is it by knowledge, by induftry, by patience, by felf-denial, or by virtue of any kind ? As all his words, as all his motions are attended to, he learns an habitual regard to every circumftance of ordinary behaviour, and ftudies to perform all thofe fmall duties, with the moft exact propriety. As he is confcious how much he is obferved, and how much mankind are difpofed to favour all his inclinations, he acts, upon the moft indifferent occafions, with that freedom and elegance, which the tho't of this naturally infpires. His air, his manner, his deportment, all mark that elegant and graceful fenfe of his own fuperiority, which thofe who are born to inferior ftations, can hardly expect to arrive at. Thefe are the arts, by which he propofes to make mankind fubmit to his authority, and to govern their inclinations according to his own pleafure ; and in this he is feldom difappointed. Thefe arts, fupported by rank and preeminence, are, upon ordinary occafions, fufficient to govern the world.

" But it is not by accomplifhments of this kind, that the man of inferior rank muft hope to diftinguifh himfelf. Politenefs is fo much the virtue of the great, that it will do little honor to any body but themfelves. The coxcomb, who imitates their manner, and affects to be eminent by
the

the fuperior propriety of his ordinary behaviour, is rewarded with a double fhare of contempt for his folly and prefumption. Why fhould the man whom nobody thinks it worth while to look at, be very anxious about the manner in which he holds up his head, or difpofes of his arms, while he walks through a room? He is occupied fure-ly with a very fuperfluous attention, and with an attention too that marks a fenfe of his own importance, which no other mortal can go along with. The moft perfect modefty and plainnefs, joined to as much negligence, as is confiftent with the refpect due to the company, ought to be the chief characteriftics of the behaviour of a private man. If ever he hopes to diftinguifh himfelf, it muft be by more important virtues: he muft ac-quire dependants, to balance the dependants of the great; and he has no other fund to pay them from but the labour of his body, and the activity of his mind. He muft cultivate thefe, therefore, he muft acquire fuperior knowledge in his pro-feffion, and fuperior induftry in the exercife of it; he muft be patient in labour, refolute in dan-ger, and firm in diftrefs. Thefe talents he muft bring into view, by the difficulty, importance, and at the fame time, good judgment of his under-takings, and by the fevere and unrelenting ap-plication with which he purfues them. Probity and prudence, generofity and franknefs, muft characterife his behaviour upon all ordinary oc-cafions; and he muft at the fame time, be for-ward to engage in all thofe fituations, in which it requires the greateft talents and virtues to act with propriety; but in which the greateft applaufe is to be acquired by thofe who can acquit them-felves with honor. With what impatience does

I   the

the man of fpirit and ambition, who is depreffed by his fituation, look round for fome great opportunity to diftinguifh himfelf? No circumftances, which can afford this, appear to him undefirable; he even looks forward with fatisfaction to the profpect of foreign war, or civil diffention; and with fecret tranfport and delight, fees, thro' all the confufion and bloodfhed which attend them, the probability of all thofe wifhed-for occafions, prefenting themfelves, in which he may draw upon himfelf the attention and admiration of mankind. The man of rank and diftinction, on the contrary, whofe whole glory confifts in the propriety of his ordinary behaviour; who is contented with the humble renown which this can afford him, and has no talents to acquire any other; is unwilling to embarrafs himfelf with what can be attended either with difficulty or diftrefs: To figure at a ball is his great triumph —he has an averfion to all public confufions, not from want of courage, for in that he is feldom defective, but from a confcioufnefs that he poffeffes none of the virtues which are required in fuch fituations, and that the public attention will certainly be drawn away from him by others: he may be willing to expofe himfelf to fome little danger, and to make a campaign, when it happens to be the fafhion; but he fhudders with horror at the thought of any fituation which demands the continual and long exertion of patience, induftry, fortitude, and long application of thought. Thefe virtues are hardly ever to be met with in men who are born to thofe high ftations. In all governments, accordingly, even in monarchies, the higheft offices are generally poffeffed, and the whole detail of the adminiftration conducted

conducted by men, who were educated in the middle and inferior ranks of life, who have been carried forward by their own induſtry and abilities, though loaded with the jealouſy, and oppoſed by the reſentment of all thoſe who were born their ſuperiors, and to whom the great, after having regarded them, firſt with contempt, and afterwards with envy, are at laſt contented to truckle with the ſame abject meanneſs, with which they deſire that the reſt of mankind ſhould behave to themſelves.

" It is the loſs of this eaſy empire over the affections of mankind, which renders the fall from greatneſs ſo inſupportable. When the family of the King of Macedon was led in triumph by Paulus Æmilius, their misfortunes, made them divide with their conqueror, the attention of the Roman people. The ſight of the royal children, whoſe tender age rendered them inſenſible of their ſituation, ſtruck the ſpectators, amidſt the public rejoicings and proſperity, with the tendereſt ſorrow and compaſſion. The King appeared next in the proceſſion—and ſeemed like one confounded and aſtoniſhed, and bereft of all ſentiment, by the greatneſs of his calamities. His friends and miniſters followed after him. As they moved along, they often caſt their eyes upon their fallen ſovereign, and always burſt into tears at the ſight—their whole behaviour demonſtrating that they thought not of their own misfortunes, but were occupied intirely by the ſuperior greatneſs of his. The generous Romans, on the contrary, beheld him with diſdain and indignation, and regarded as unworthy of all compaſſion the man who could be ſo mean ſpirited as to bear to live under ſuch calamities. Yet

what

what did thofe calamities amount to ? He was to
fpend the remainder of his days, in a ftate, which
of itfelf fhould feem worthy of envy ; a ftate of
plenty, eafe, leifure and fecurity, from which it
was impoffible for him, even by his own folly, to
fall. But he was no longer to be furrounded by
that admiring mob of fools, flatterers, and dependants, who had formerly been accuftomed to
attend all his motions ; he was no longer to be
gazed upon by multitudes, nor to have it in his
power to render himfelf the object of their refpect, their gratitude, their love, and their admiration. The paffions of nature were no longer
to mould themfelves upon his inclinations. This
was that infupportable calamity, which bereaved
the king of all fentiment ; which made his friends
forget their own misfortunes, and which the Roman magnanimity could fcarce conceive how a-
ny man could be fo mean fpirited as to bear to
furvive.

" To thofe who have been accuftomed to the
poffeffion, or even to the hope of public admiration, all other pleafures ficken and decay.

" Of fuch mighty importance does it appear
to be in the imaginations of men, to ftand in
that fituation which fets them moft in the view
of general fympathy, and attention ; and thus
place, that great object which divides the wives
of aldermen, is the end of half the labours of
human life ; and is the caufe of all the tumult
and buftle, all the rapine and injuftice, which a-
varice and ambition have introduced into this
world. People of fenfe, it is faid indeed, defpife
place ; that is to fay they defpife fetting at the
head of the table, and are indifferent who it is
that is pointed out to the company by that frivolous

volous circumftance which the fmalleft advantage
is capable of overballancing.   But rank, diftinction, pre-eminence, no man defpifes."

No. 11.

Heroes proceed ! What bounds your pride fhall hold?
What check reftrain your thirft of power and gold?

THE anfwer to the queftion, in the motto,
can be none other than this, that as nature has
eftablifhed in the bofoms of heroes no limits to
thofe paffions ; and as the world, inftead of re-
ftraining encourages them, the check muft be, in
the form of government.

The world encourages ambitiou and avarice,
by taking the moft decided part in their favor.
The Roman world approved of the ambition of
Cæfar ; and, notwithftanding all the pains that
have been taken with fo much reafon, by moral
and political writers to difgrace it, the world has
approved it thefe feventeen hundred years; and ftill
efteems his name an honor to the firft empire in
Europe.   Confider the ftory of the ambition and
the fall of Cardinal Wolfey, and Archbifhop Laud ;
the indignation of the world againft their tyranny has been very faint ; the fympathy with their
fall has been very ftrong.   Confider all the examples in hiftory of fuccefsful ambition, you will
find none generally condemned by mankind ; on
the other hand, think of the inftances of ambition, unfuccefsful and difappointed ; or of falls
from

from great heights, you find the fympathy of the world univerfally affected. Cruelty and tyranny of the blackeft kind muft accompany the ftory, to deftroy or fenfibly diminifh this pity. That world, for the regulations of whofe prejudices, paffions, imaginations and interefts, governments are inftituted, is fo unjuft, that neither religion, natural nor revealed, nor any thing, but a well ordered and well balanced government has ever been able to correct it, and that but imperfectly. It is as true in modern London, as it was in ancient Rome, that the fympathy of the world is lefs excited by the deftruction of the houfe of a man of merit, in obfcurity, or even in middle life, though it be by the unjuft violence of men, than by the fame calamity befalling a rich man, by the righteous indignation of heaven.

> Nil habuit Codrus: quis enim negat? et tamen illud
> Perdidit infelix totum nil: ultimus autem
> Ærumnæ cumulus, quod nudum et frufta rogantem
> Nemo cibo, nemo hofpitio tectoque juvabit.
> Si magna Arturi cecidit domus, horrida mater,
> Pullati proceres, differt vadimonia Prætor :
> Tunc gemimus cafus urbis, tunc odimus ignem.
> Ardet adhuc, et jam, accurrit qui marmora donet,
> Conferat impenfas. Hic nuda et candida figna ;
> Hic aliquid præclarum Euphranoris et Polycleti,
> Hic phæcafianorum vetera ornamenta Deorum.
> Hic libros dabit et forulos, mediamque Minervam ;
> Hic modium argenti : meliora et plura reponit
> Perficus orborum lautiffimus, ut merito jam
> Sufpectus, tanquam ipfe fuas incenderit ædes.
> But hark ! th' affrighted crowd's tumultuous cries
> Roll through the ftreets, and thunder to the fkies :
> Rais'd from fome pleafing dream of wealth and power,
> Some pompous palace, or fome blifsful bower,
> Aghaft you ftart, and fcarce with aching fight,
> Suftain the approaching fire's tremendous light ;
> Swift from purfuing horrors take your way,
> And leave your little all to flames a prey ;

Then

Then thro' the world a wretched vagrant roam,
For where can ftarving merit find a home?
In vain your mournful narrative difclofe,
While all neglect, and moft infult your woes.
———— ——— ——— But
Should heavn's juft bolts Orgilio's wealth confound
And fpread his flaming palace on the ground,
Swift o'er the land the difmal rumour flies,
And public mournings pacify the fkies;
The Laureat tribe in venal verfe relate,
How virtue wars with perfecuting fate;
With well-feign'd gratitude the penfion'd band
Refund the plunder of the beggar'd land.
See! while he builds, the gaudy vaffals come,
And crowd with fudden wealth the rifing dome;
The price of boroughs and of fouls reftore;
And raife his treafures higher than before:
Now blefs'd with all the baubles of the great,
The polifh'd marble and the fhining plate,
Orgilio fees the golden pile afpire,
And hopes from angry heav'n another fire.

Although the verfe, both of the Roman and
the Briton, is fatire, its keeneft feverity confifts
in its truth.

———————————

No. 12.

———

Order is Heaven's firft law—and this confefs'd,
Some are, and muft be, greater than the reft :
More rich, more wife—But who infers from hence,
That fuch are happier, fhocks all common fenfe.

THE world is fenfible of the neceffity of fupporting their favourites under the firft onfets of
misfortune—left the fall fhould be dreadful and
irrecoverable—for according to the great Mafter
of Nature,   'Tis

'Tis certain, greatnefs, once fallen out with fortune,
Muft fall out with men too : What the declin'd is
He fhall as foon read in the eyes of others,
As feel in his own fall : for men, like butterflies,
Shew not their mealy wings but to the fummer ;
And not a man for being fingly man,
Hath any honor ; but's honor'd for thofe honors
That are without him, as place, riches, favor,
Prizes of accident as oft as merit.

Mankind are fo fenfible of thefe things, that
by a kind of inftinct or intuition, they generally
follow the advice of the fame author.

Take the inftant way,
For honor travels in a ftraight fo narrow
Where one but goes abreaft : Keep then the path,
For emulation hath a thoufand fons,
That one by one purfue ; if you give way,
Or hedge afide from the direct forth-right,
Like to an enter'd tide, they all rufh by,
And leave you hindmoft ;
Or like a gallant horfe, fall'n in firft rank,
Lie there for pavement to the abject rear,
O'errun and trampled on.

The inference from all the contemplations and
experiments which have been made, by all nations, upon thefe difpofitions to imitation, emulation, and rivalry, is expreffed by the fame great
teacher of morality and politics.

Degree being vizarded,
Th' unworthieft fhews as fairly in the mafk.
The Heaven's themfelves, the Planets and this centre,
Obferve degree, priority and place,
Infifture, courfe, proportion, feafon, form,
Office and cuftom, in all line of order :
And therefore is the glorious planet Sol,
In noble eminence, enthron'd and fpher'd
Amidft the others ; whofe med'cinable eye
Corrects the ill afpects of planets evil,
And pofts like the commandment of a King,

Sans

Sans check, to good and bad ; but when the planets
In evil mixture, to diforder wander,
What plagues and what portents ! what mutiny !
What raging of the fea ! Shaking of earth !
Commotion in the winds ! Frights, changes, horrors,
Divert and crack, rend and deracinate,
The unity and married calm of States,
Quite from their fixure ? O,'when Degree is fhak'd,
Which is the ladder to all high defigns,
The enterprize is fick ! How could communities;
Degrees in fchools, and brotherhoods in cities,
The primogenitive and due of birth,
Prerogative of age, crowns, fceptres, laurels,
But by Degree ftand in authentic place ?
Take but Degree away ; untune that ftring
And hark ! what difcord follows ! each thing meets
In meer oppugnancy : the bounded waters
Should lift their bofoms, higher than the fhores,
And make a fop, of all this folid globe :
Strength fhould be lord of imbecility,
And the rude fon fhould ftrike his father dead :
Force fhould be right ; or rather right and wrong
Should lofe their names, and fo fhould juftice too.
Then every thing includes itfelf in power,
Power into will, will into appetite ;
And appetite an univerfal wolf,
Muft make perforce an univerfal prey,
And laft eat up himfelf.
This chaos, when Degree is fuffocate
Follows the choaking.
　　　　　　The General's difdain'd,
By him one ftep below : he by the next ;
That next by him beneath : fo every ftep
Exampled by the firft pace, that is fick
Of his fuperior, grows to an envious fever
Of pale and bloodlefs emulation.
Troy in our weaknefs ftands, not in her ftrength.
Moft wifely hath Ulyffes here difcovered
The Fever, whereof all our power is fick.

K　　　　　　　　No.

No. 13.

Think We, like fome weak Prince, th' eternal caufe
Prone, for his fav'rites, to reverfe his laws ?

EMULATION, which is imitation and fomething more—a defire not only to equal or refemble, but to excel is fo natural a movement
of the human heart, that, wherever men are to
be found, and in whatever manner affociated or
connected, we fee its effects. They are not more
affected by it, as individuals, than they are in
communities. There are rivalries between every
little fociety in the fame city—between familīes
and all the connections by confanguinity and affini-
ty—between trades, faculties, and profeffions--be-
tween congregations, parifhes and churches—between fchools, colleges, and univerfities—between diftricts, villages, cities, provinces and nations.

National rivalries are more frequently the caufe
of wars than the ambition of minifters, or the
pride of kings.—As long as there is patriotifm,
there will be national emulation, vanity and pride.
It is national pride which commonly ftimulates
kings and minifters.—National fear, apprehenfion of danger, and the neceffity of felf-defence,
is added to fuch rivalries for wealth, confideration and power. The fafety, independence, and
exiftence of a nation, depends upon keeping up
an high fenfe of its own honor, dignity and power in the hearts of its individuals, and a lively
jealoufy of the growing power and afpiring ambition

bition of a neighbouring State.—This is well illuftrated in the Political Geography, publifhed in our newfpapers from London, within a few weeks. " The jealoufies and enmities, the alliances and friendfhips, or rather the combinations of different States and Princes. might almoft be learned from a map, without attention to what has paffed, or is now paffing in the world. Next neighbours are political enemies : States between which a common neighbor, and therefore a common enemy intervenes, are good friends. In this refpect Europe may be compared to a chefs board, marked with the black, and with the white fpots of political difcord and concord.— Before the union between England and Scotland, a friendfhip and alliance fubfifted for centuries, between the latter of thefe kingdoms and France, becaufe they were both inimical to England. For a like reafon, before a Prince of Bourbon, in the beginning of the prefent century, was raifed to the Spanifh throne, a good underftanding fubfifted for the moft part, between England and Spain, and before the late alliance, there was peace and kindnefs, with little interruption. for the fpace of centuries, between England and the Emperor. An alliance has long fubfifted between the French and the Turks, on account of the intervening dominion of the Auftrians. The Swedes were long the friends of France, on account of the intervention of Holland and Denmark—and becaufe Sweden, the friend of France, was fituated in the neighborhood of the Ruffian territories, a friendfhip and commercial intercourfe was eftablifhed, from the very firft time that Mufcovy appears on the political theatre of Europe, between England and Ruffia. It is fuperfluous to multiply inftan-

ces

ces of this kind. All paft hiftory and prefent obfervation will confirm the truth of our pofition
—which, though very fimple, is like all other
fimple truths, of very great importance—for,
however the accidental caprices and paffions of
individual Princes, or their minifters, may alter
the relative difpofitions and interefts of nations
for a time, there is a natural tendency to revert
to the alteration already defcribed. We have
been led into thefe reflections by the treaty offenfive and defenfive, that has been formed between Sweden, Pruffia, and the Sublime Porte—
between Pruffia and Holland—and the report
which is very probable, that a treaty offenfive and
defenfive is on the point of being concluded between Turkey and Poland. In this chain of alliances we find the order of the chefsboard adhered to, in fome inftances, but paffed over in
others. It is obferved there fhould be an alliance between Ruffia and Sweden—and alfo that
there fhould be an alliance between Poland and
Turkey, becaufe Ruffia intervenes between Turkey and Sweden, and Hungary between Turkey
and Poland—but that there fhould be an alliance
between Poland and Pruffia is owing to particular and accidental circumftances. The two former alliances may therefore be expected to be
lafting—the latter to be only temporary and pre-
carious. In general the chain of alliance, that
is formed or forming, among the Swedes, Pruf-
fians, Poles, Dutch, Turks, and we may fay the
Englifh, is a moft ftriking proof, of the real or
fuppofed ftrength and influence of the two imperial courts of Ruffia and Germany."

The writer of this paragraph might have added
the alliance between England and Portugal, and
that

that between the United States of America and France. The principle of all thefe examples is as natural as emulation, and as infallible as the fincerity of intereft. On it, turns the whole fyftem of human affairs. The Congrefs of 1776 were fully aware of it. With no fmall degree of vehemence, was it urged, as an argument for the declaration of Independence : with confidence and firmnefs wasit foretold, that France couldnot avoid accepting the propofitions that fhould be made to her ; that the Court of Verfailles could not anfwer it, to her own fubjects, and that all Europe would pronounce her blind, loft and undone, if fhe rejected fo fair an opportunity of difembarraffing herfelf, from the danger of fo powerful and hoftile a rival, whofe naval fuperiority held all her foreign dominions, her maritime power and commercial intereft, at mercy.

But why all this of Emulation and Rivalry ?—Becaufe, as the whole hiftory of the civil wars of France, given us by *Davila*, is no more than a relation of rivalries, fucceeding each other in a rapid feries, the reflections we have made will affift us, both to underftand that noble hiftorian, and to form a right judgment of the ftate of affairs in France at the prefent moment. They will fuggeft alfo to *Americans*, efpecially to thofe who have been unfriendly, and may be now lukewarm to their national Conftitution, fome ufeful enquiries, fuch as thofe for examples : Whether ttere are not emulations, of a ferious complexion among ourfelves ? between cities and univerfities ? between North and South ? The Middle and the North ? The Middle and the South ? between one ftate and another ? between the governments of States and the National Government ?

ment? and between individual patriots and heroes in all thefe? What is the natural remedy againſt the inconveniences and dangers of thefe rivalries? Whether a well-balanced Conſtitution—fuch as that of our Union purports to be, ought not to be cordially fupported, till its defects, if it has any, can be corrected, by every good citizen, as our only hope of peace, and our ark of fafety?—But it muſt be left to the contemplations of our State Phyſicians to difcover the caufes and the remedy of that "*fever, whereof our power is fick.*" One queſtion only ſhall be refpectfully infinuated : Whether equal laws, the refult only of a balanced government, can ever be obtained and preferved without fome figns or other of diſtinction and degree?

We are told that our friends, the National Affembly of France, have aboliſhed all diſtinctions. But be not deceived, my dear countrymen. Impoffibilities cannot be performed. Have they levelled all fortunes, and equally divided all property? Have they made all men and women equally wife, elegant, and beautiful? Have they annihilated the names of Bourbon and Montmorency, Rochefoucalt and Noailles, La Fayette and La Moignon, Neckar and de la Calonne, Mirabeau and Bailey? Have they committed to the flames all the records, annals and hiſtories of the nation? All the copies of Mezerai, Daniel, de Thou, Veilly, and a thoufand others? Have they burned all their pictures, and broken all their ſtatues? Have they blotted out of all memories, the names, places of abode, and illuſtrious actions of all their anceſtors? Have they not ſtill Princes of the firſt and fecond order, Nobles and Knights? Have they no record nor memory who are the men, who

who compofe the prefent National Affembly ?—
Do they wifh to have that diftinction forgotten ?
Have the French officers who ferved in America
melted their Eagles, and torn their ribbons ?

No. 14.

'Tis with our judgments as our watches—none
Go juft alike, yet each believes his own.

ALL the miracles enumerated in our laft number, muft be performed in France, before all diftinctions can be annihilated, and diftinctions in
abundance would be found, after all, for French
gentlemen, in the hiftory of England, Holland,
Spain, Germany, Italy, America, and all other
countries on the globe.

The wifdom of nations has remarked the univerfal confideration paid to wealth ; and that the
paffion of avarice, excited by it, produced trea-
chery, cowardice, and a felfifh unfocial meannefs,
but had no tendency to produce thofe virtues of
patience, courage, fortitude, honor, or patriotifm,
which the fervice of the public required in their
citizens, in peace and war.

The wifdom of nations has obferved, that the
general attention paid to birth, produced a different kind of fentiments ; thofe of pride in the
maxims and principles in religion, morals and government, as well as in the talents and virtues
which firft produced illuftration to anceftors.

As

As the pride of wealth produced nothing but meannefs of fentiment, and a fordid fcramble for money; and the pride of birth produced fome degree of emulation in knowledge and virtue; the wifdom of nations has endeavoured to employ one prejudice to counteract another; the prejudice in favor of birth, to moderate, correct, and reftrain the prejudice in favor of wealth.

The National Affembly of France is too enlightened a body to overlook the enquiry. What effect on the moral character of the nation would be produced, by deftroying, if that were poffible, all attention to families, and fetting all the paffions on the purfuit of gain. Whether univerfal venality, and an incorrigible corruption in elections would not be the neceffary confequence. It may be relied on, however, that the intentions of that auguft and magnanimous affembly, are mifunderftood and mifreprefented. Time will develope their defigns, will fhew them to be more judicious than to attempt impoffibilities fo obvious, as that of the abolition of all diftinctions.

ALPHONSUS the tenth, the aftronomical king of Caftile, has been accufed of impiety, for faying that "if, at the time of the creation, he had been called to the councils of the divinity, he could have given fome ufeful advice, concerning the motions of the ftars." It is not probable, that any thing was intended by him, more than an humorous farcafm, or a fneer of contempt, at the Ptolemaic fyftem, a projection of which he had before him. But if the National Affembly fhould have ferioufly in contemplation, and fhould refolve in earneft the total abolition of all diftinctions and orders, it would be much more difficult to vindicate them from an accufation of impiety.

piety. God, in the conftitution of nature, has ordained that every man fhall have a difpofition to emulation, as well as imitation, and confequently a paffion for diftinction, and that all men fhall not have equal means and opportunities of gratifying it. Shall we believe the National Affembly capable of refolving that no man fhall have any defire of diftinction ; or that all men fhall have equal means of gratifying it ?— Or that no man fhall have any means of gratifying it ? What would this be better than faying, "if we had been called to the councils of the celeftials, we could have given better advice in the conftitution of human nature ?" If nature and that affembly, could be thus at variance, which however is not credible, the world would foon fee, which is the moft powerful.

That there is already a fciffion, in the National Affembly, like all others, paft, prefent, and to come, is moft certain. There is an ariftocratical party, a democratical party, an armed neutrality, and moft probably a monarchial party : befides another divifion, who muft finally prevail, or liberty will be loft : I mean a fet of members, who are equal friends to monarchy, ariftrocracy, and democracy, and wifh for an equal independent mixture of all three in their conftitution. Each of thefe parties has its chief, and thefe chiefs are or will be rivals. Religion will be both the object and the pretext of fome : liberty, of others : fubmiffion and obedience of others : and leveling, downright levelling, of not a few. But the attention, confideration and congratulations of the public, will be the object of all. Situation and office will be aimed at by fome of all parties. Contefts and diffentions will arife between thefe runners in the fame race. The natural and ufual

progrefs,

progrefs, is, from debate in the affembly to dif-
cuffions in print ; from the fearch of truth and
public utility in both, to fophiftry and the fpirit
of party : Evils fo greatly dreaded by the ingenu-
ous " Citizen of New-Heaven," to whom we
have now the honor of paying our firft refpects,
hoping that hereafter we may find an opportunity to make him our more particular compli-
ments.* From fophiftry and party fpirit, the
tranfition is quick and eafy to falfhood, impof-
ture, and every fpecies of artificial evolution and
criminal intrigue. As unbalanced parties of
every defcription, can never tolerate a free enquiry of any kind, when employed againft themfelves, the licence, and even the moft temperate
freedom of the prefs, foon excites refentment and
revenge. A writer, unpopular with an oppofite
party, becaufe he is too formidable in wit or argument, may firft be burnt in effigy : or a printer
may have his office affaulted : cuffs and kicks,
boxes and cudgels, are heard of, among plebeian
ftatefmen ; challenges and fingle combats among
the ariftocratic legiflators—Riots and feditions
at length break men's bones, or flea off their fkins.
Lives are loft : and when blood is once drawn,
men, like other animals, become outrageous : If
one party has not a fuperiority over the other,
clear enough to decide every thing at its pleafure,
a civil war enfues. When the nation arrives at
this period of the progreffion, every leader, at
the head of his votaries, even if you admit him
to have the beft intentions in the world, will find
himfelf compelled to form them into fome military arrangement, both for offence and defence ; to
                                                    build

* Alluding to four Letters publifhed about that time, by Condorcet,
who called himfelf a Citizen of New Heaven, in which he recommended
a Government in a Single Affembly, which was accordingly adopted, and
ruined France.

build caftles and fortify eminences, like the feudal Barons. For ariftocratical rivalries and democratical rivalries too, when unbalanced againft each other, by fome third mediating power, natu-rally and unfailingly produce a feudal fyftem.— If this fhould be the courfe in France, the poor, deluded, and devoted partizans would foon be fond enough of decorating their leaders, with the old titles of dukes, marquiffes and counts, or doing any thing elfe, to increafe the power of their commander over themfelves, to unite their wills and forces for their own fafety and defence, or to give him weight with their enemies.*

The men of letters in France, are wifely re-forming one feudal fyftem; but may they not unwifely, lay the foundation of another? A le-giflature in one affembly, can have no other ter-mination than in civil diffention, feudal anarchy, or fimple monarchy. The beft apology which can be made for their frefh attempt of a fove-reignty in one affembly, an idea at leaft as ancient in France as *Stephen Boetius*, is, that it is only in-tended to be momentary. If a fenate had been propofed, it muft have been formed, moft proba-bly of Princes of the blood, Cardinals, Arch-bifhops, Dukes and Marquiffes, and all thefe to-gether would have obftructed the progrefs of the reformation in religion and government, and procured an abortion, to the regeneration of France. Pennfylvania eftablifhed her fingle af-fembly in 1776, upon the fame principle. An apprehenfion that the Proprietary and Quaker interefts would prevail, to the election of charac-ters difaffected to the American caufe, finally pre-ponderated againft two legiflative councils. Penn-fylvania, and Georgia, who followed her example, have found by experience, the neceffity of a change

* This has all been accomplifhed in the new Emperor Napoleon. 1804.

change : and France, by the fame infallible progrefs of reafoning, will difcover the fame neceffity :
Happy indeed, if the experiment fhall not coft
her more dear.   That the fubject is confidered
in this light, by the beft friends of liberty in
Europe, appears by the words of Dr. Price, lately
publifhed in this paper.—" Had not the ariftocratical and clerical orders," fays that fage and
amiable writer, " have been obliged to throw
themfelves into one chamber with the commons,
no reformation could have taken place, and the
regeneration of the kingdom would have been
impoffible.   And in future legiflatures, were
thefe two orders to make diftinct and independent
ftates, all that has been done would probably be
foon undone.   Hereafter, perhaps, when the new
conftitution, as now formed, has acquired ftrength
by time, the National Affembly may find it prac-
ticable as well as expedient, to eftablifh by means
of a third Eftate, fuch a check, as now takes place
in the American government, and is indifpenfible
in the Britifh government."*

No. 15.

Firft follow nature, and your judgment frame
By her juft ftandard, which is ftill the fame.

THE world grows more enlightened : Knowledge is more equally diffufed : News-papers,
Magazines, and circulating libraries, have made
mankind wifer : Titles and diftinctions, ranks
and

* It is to be lamented that the Doctor had not lived to 1804, to fee the
errors into which his honeft enthufiafm betrayed him.

and orders, parade and ceremony, are all going
out of fashion. This is roundly and frequently
asserted in the streets, and sometimes on theatres
of higher *rank*.   Some truth there is in it : and if
the opportunity were temperately improved, to
the reformation of abuses, the rectification of errors, and the dissipation of pernicious prejudices,
a great advantage it might be.   But, on the o-
ther hand, false inferences may be drawn from it,
which may make mankind wish for the age of
Dragons, Giants and Fairies.   If all decorum,
discipline and subordination are to be destroyed,
and universal pyrrhonism, anarchy, and insecuri-
ty of property are to be introduced, nations will
soon wish their books in ashes, seek for darkness
and ignorance, superstition and fanaticism, as
blessings, and follow the standard of the first mad
despot, who, with the enthusiasm of another
Mahomet, will endeavour to obtain them.

Are riches, honors, and beauty going out of
fashion ? Is not the rage for them, on the contrary, increased faster than improvement, in knowledge ? As long as either of these are in vogue,
will there not be emulations and rivalries ? Does
not the increase of knowledge in any man, increase his emulation ; and the diffusion of knowledge among men, multiply rivalries ? Has the
progress of science, arts and letters, yet discover-
ed that there are no passions in human nature ?
No ambition, avarice or a desire of fame ? Are
these passions cooled, diminished or extinguished ?
Is the rage for admiration less ardent in men or
women ? Have these propensities less a tendency
to divisions, controversies, seditions, mutinies,
and civil wars, than formerly ? On the contrary,
the more knowledge is diffused, the more the
passions are extended, and the more furious they
grow ?

grow? Had Cicero lefs vanity, or Cæfar lefs ambition, for their vaft erudition? Had the King of
Pruffia lefs of one, than the other? There
is no connection in the mind between fcience and
paffion, by which the former can extinguifh or
diminifh the latter : it on the contrary fometimes
increafes them, by giving them exercife. Were
the paffions of the Romans lefs vivid, in the age
of Pompey, than in the time of Mummius? Are
thofe of the Britons, more moderate at this hour
than in the reigns of the Tudors? Are the paffions
of Monks, the weaker for all their learning? Are
not jealoufy, envy, hatred, malice and revenge,
as well as emulation and ambition, as rancorous
in the cells of Carmelites, as in the courts of
Princes? Go to the Royal Society of London :
is there lefs emulation for the chair of Sir Ifaac
Newton, than there was, and commonly will be
for all elective prefidencies? Is there lefs animofity and rancour, arifing from mutual emulations
in that region of fcience, than there is among
the moft ignorant of mankind? Go to Paris :
how do you find the men of letters? united,
friendly, harmonious, meek, humble, modeft,
charitable? prompt to mutual forbearance? un-
affuming? ready to acknowledge fuperior merit?
zealous to encourage the firft fymptoms of
genius? Afk Voltaire and Roffeau, Marmontel
and De Mably.*

The increafe and diffemination of knowledge,
inftead of rendering unneceffary, the checks of
emulation and the balances of rivalry, in the orders of fociety and conftitution of government,
augment the neceffity of both. It becomes the
more

* The envy, jealoufy, rivalries, factions, cabals, intrigues and animofities, among the men of letters in Paris, were as violent at leaft as they
were at Court, and as furious, tho' not fo bloody as they were among the
people and their government, under any form of their variable conftitutions from 1786 to 1804.

more indifpenfable, that every man fhould know his place and be made to keep it. Bad men increafe in knowledge as faft as good men, and fcience, arts, tafte, fenfe and letters, are employed for the purpofes of injuftice and tyranny, as well as thofe of law and liberty; for corruption as well as for virtue.

FRENCHMEN! Act and think like yourfelves! confeffing human nature, be magnanimous and wife. Acknowledging and boafting yourfelves to be men, avow the feelings of men. The affectation of being exempted from paffions, is inhuman. The grave pretention to fuch fingularity is folemn hypocrify. Both are unworthy of your frank and generous natures. Confider that government is intended to fet bounds to paffions which nature has not limited: and to affift reafon, confcience, juftice and truth in controuling interefts, which, without it, would be as unjuft as uncontroulable.

AMERICANS! rejoice, that from experience, you have learned wifdom: and inftead of whimfical and fantaftical projects, you have adopted a promifing effay, towards a well ordered government. Inftead of following any foreign example, to return to *the legiflation of confufion*, contemplate the means of reftoring decency, honefty and order in fociety, by preferving, and compleating, if any thing fhould be found neceffary to compleat, the balance of your government. In a well balanced government, reafon, confcience, truth and virtue muft be refpected by all parties, and exerted for the public good. Advert to the principles on which you commenced that glorious felf defence, which, if you behave with fteadinefs and confiftency, may ultimately loofen the chains of all mankind. If you will take the trouble

trouble to read over the memorable proceedings
of the town of Bofton, on the 28th day of October
ber 1772, when the Committee of Correfpondence of twenty one perfons, was appointed to
ftate the rights of the Colonifts as men, as chrift-
ians and as fubjects, and to publifh them to the
world, with the infringements and violations of
them, you will find the great principles of civil
and religious liberty, for which you have contended fo fuccefsfully, and which the world is
contending for after your example. I could
tranfcribe with pleafure, the whole of this immortal pamphlet, which is a real picture of the
fun of liberty, rifing on the human race : but
fhall felect only a few words, more directly to the
prefent purpofe. " The firft fundamental pofitive
law of all commonwealths or ftates, is the eftablifhment of the legiflative power." Page 9.

" It is abfolutely neceffary, in a mixed government, like that of this Province, that a *due proportion*, or *balance* of power fhould be eftablifhed
among the feveral branches of the legiflative.
Our anceftors received from King William and
Queen Mary, a charter, by which it was underftood by both parties in the contract, that fuch a
proportion or balance was fixed ; and therefore
every thing which renders any one branch of the
legiflative more independent of the other two,
than it was originally defigned, is an alteration
of the Conftitution."

AMERICANS! In your Congrefs at Philadelphia,
on Friday, the 14th day of October, 1774, you
laid down the fundamental principles, for which
you were about to contend, and from which it
is to be hoped you will never depart. For afferting and vindicating your rights and liberties, you
declared,

declared, " That by the immutable laws of nature, the principles of the Englifh Conftitution,
and your feveral charters or compacts, you were
entitled to life, liberty and property ; that your
anceftors were entitled to all the rights, liberties
and immunities of free and natural born fubjects
in England : that you, their defcendants, were
entitled to the exercife and enjoyment of all fuch
of them as your local and other circumftances,
enabled you to exercife and enjoy. That the
foundation of Englifh liberty, and of all free
governments, is, a right in the people, to partici-
pate in their legiflative council. That you were
entitled to the common law of England, and
more efpecially to the great and ineftimable
privilege of being tried by your peers of the vici-
nage, according to the courfe of that law. *That
it is indifpenfably neceffary to good government, and
rendered effential by the Englifh Conftitution, that the
conftituent branches of the legiflature, be independent
of each other.*" Thefe, among others, you then
claimed, demanded and infifted on, as your in-
dubitable rights and liberties. Thefe are the
principles, on which you firft united and affociated, and if you fteadily and confiftently maintain
them, they will not only fecure freedom and
happinefs to yourfelves and your pofterity, but
your example will be imitated by all Europe, and
in time perhaps by all mankind. The nations
are in travail, and great events muft have birth.
" The minds of men are in movement from the
Borifthenes to the Atlantic. Agitated with new
and ftrong emotions, they fwell and heave beneath
oppreffion, as the feas within the polar circle, at
the approach of fpring. The genius of philofophy, with the touch of Ithuriel's fpear, is trying

the

the eftablifhments of the earth. The various forms of prejudice, fuperftition and fervility, ftart up, in their true fhapes, which had long impofed upon the world, under the revered femblances of honor, faith and loyalty. Whatever is loofe muft be fhaken; whatever is corrupted muft be lopt away; whatever is not built on the broad bafis of public utility, muft be thrown to the ground. Obfcure murmurs gather and fwell into a tempeft; the fpirit of enquiry like a fevere and fearching wind, penetrates every part of the great body politic; and whatever is unfound, what-ever is infirm, fhrinks at the vifitation. Liberty, led by philofophy, diffufes her bleffings to every clafs of men; and even extends a fmile of hope and promife to the poor African, the victim of hard impenetrable avarice. Man, as man, be-comes an object of refpect. Tenets are transfer-ed, from theory to practice. The glowing fen-timent, the lofty fpeculation, no longer ferve " but to adorn the pages of a book:" they are brought home to men's bufinefs and bofoms; and what fome centuries ago, it was daring but to think, and dangerous to exprefs, is now realized and carried into effect. Syftems are analyfed into their firft principles, and principles are fairly purfued to their legitimate confequences."

This is all enchanting.—But amidft our enthu-fiafm, there is great reafon to paufe, and preferve our fobriety. It is true, that the firft empire of the world is breaking the fetters of human reafon and exerting the energies of redeemed liberty. In the glowing ardor of her zeal, fhe condef-cends, AMERICANS, to pay the moft fcrupulous attention to your maxims, principles and exam-ple. There is reafon to fear fhe has copied from
you

you errors, which have coft you very dear. Affift her, by your example, to rectify them before they involve her in calamities, as much greater than yours, as her population is more unwieldy, and her fituation more expofed to the baleful influence of rival neighbours. Amidft all their exultations, AMERICANS and FRENCHMEN fhould remember, that the perfectability of man, is only human and terreftial perfectability. Cold will ftill freeze, and fire will never ceafe to burn ; difeafe and vice will continue to diforder, and death to terrify mankind. Emulation next to felf prefervation will forever be the great fpring of human actions, and the balance of a well ordered government, will alone be able to prevent that emulation from degenerating into dangerous ambition, irregular rivalries, deftructive factions, wafting feditions, and bloo dy civil wars.

The great queftion will forever remain, *who fhall work?* Our fpecies cannot all be idle. Leifure for ftudy muft ever be the portion of a few. The number employed in government, muft forever be very fmall. Food, raiment and habitations, the indifpenfible wants of all, are not to be obtained without the continual toil of ninety-nine in an hundred of mankind. As reft is rapture to the weary man, thofe who labor little will always be envied by thofe who labor much, though the latter, in reality, be probably the moft enviable. With all the encouragements public and private, which can ever be given to general education, and it is fcarcely poffible they fhould be too many, or too great, the laboring part of the people, can never be learned. The controverfy between the rich and the poor, the laborious and the idle, the learned and the ignorant,

rant, diftinctions as old as the creation, and as
extenfive as the globe ; diftinctions which no art
or policy, no degree of virtue or philofophy can
ever wholly deftroy, will continue, and rivalries
will fpring out of them. Thefe parties will be,
reprefented in the legiflature, and muft be balanced, or one will opprefs the other. There will
never probably be found, any other mode of
eftablifhing fuch an equilibrium, than by conftituting the reprefentation of each, an independent
branch of the legiflature, and an independent
executive authority, fuch as that in our government, to be a third branch, and a mediator or an
arbitrator between them. Property muft be fecured, or liberty cannot exift : but if unlimited,
or unballanced power of difpofing property, be
put into the hands of thofe, who have no property, France will find, as we have found, the
lamb committed to the cuftody of the wolf. In
fuch a cafe, all the pathetic exhortations a nd ad-
dreffes of the National Affembly to the people, to
refpect property, will be regarded no more than
the warbles of the fongfters of the foreft. The
great art of law giving confifts in balancing the
poor againft the rich in the legiflature, and in
conftituting the legiflative, a perfect balance a-
gainft the executive power, at the fame time,
that no individual or party can become its rival.
The effence of a free government confifts in an
effectual controul of rivalries. The executive
and the legiflative powers are natural rivals ; and
if each, has not an effectual controul over the
other, the weaker, will ever be the lamb in the
paws of the wolf. The nation which will not
adopt an equilibrium of power, muft adopt a
defpotifm. There is no other alternative. Ri-
                                                valries

valries muſt be controuled, or they will throw all things into confuſion ; and there is nothing but deſpotiſm, or a balance of power, which can controul them. Even in the ſimple monarchies, the nobility and the judicatures, conſtitute a balance, though a very imperfect one, againſt the royalties.

Let us conclude with one reflection more, which ſhall barely be hinted at, as delicacy, if not prudence, may require, in this place, ſome degree of reſerve. Is there a poſſibility, that the government of nations may fall into the hands of men, who teach the moſt diſconſolate of all creeds, that men are but fire-flies, and that this *all* is without a father ? Is this the way, to make man, as man, an object of reſpect ? Or is it, to make murder itſelf, as indifferent as ſhooting a plover, and the extermination of the Rohilla nation, as innocent, as the ſwallowing of mites, on a morſel of cheeſe ? If ſuch a caſe ſhould happen, would not one of theſe, the moſt credulous of all believers, have reaſon to pray, to his eternal nature, or his almighty chance, (the more abſurdity there is in this ad reſs the more in character) *give us again the gods of the Greeks—give us again the more intelligible as well as more comfortable ſyſtems of Athanaſius and Calvin—nay, give us again our Popes and Hiearchies, Benedictines and Jeſuits, with all their ſuperſtition and fanaticiſm, impoſtures and tyranny.* A certain Dutcheſs of venerable years and maſculine underſtanding, ſaid of ſome of the Philoſophers of the eighteenth century, admirably well, " On ne croit pas, dans le Chriſt-ianiſme, mais on croit, toutes les ſottiſes poſſibles."

No.

No. 16.

Oppofant, fans relâche, avec trop de prudence,
Les *Guifes* aux *Condés*, et la France a la France.
Toujours prête á s'unir avec fes ennemis
Et changeant d'intérêt, de rivaux, et d'amis.

THE rivalry, between the houfes of Guife and
Montmorency, or in other words, the ambition
of the Cardinal de Lorrain, and the Duke of
Guife, to outſtrip the Montmorency, produced a
war. Charles the Vth. was preparing with a
numerous army to lay fiege to Metz. It was not
doubted that the conduct of fo important a war,
would be committed to one of the two favorites.
But the Conſtable Montmorency, more than
fixty years of age, preferred a refidence near the
perfon of the King, to a rifque of his reputation,
in new dangers. The Duke of Guife, on the
contrary, full of courage, and burning with ardor
to diftinguifh himfelf, folicited the command,
with the more vivacity, as he faw no other refource than in military fuccefles, to efface the
credit, and eclipfe the glory of the Conſtable. He
was therefore charged with the defence of Metz,
with the confent, or at leaſt, without the oppofition of the Conſtable, who internally, was not
difpleafed to fee his competitor, expofe his life,
or his reputation to danger. The Duke fulfilled
perfectly, the idea, which had been conceived of
his valor and prudence—uncertain as the fuccefs
of the enterprife had been, he came out of it vic-
torious, and covered with glory. This great
action did him fo much honor with the King, and
the

the whole nation, that they committed to him, in preference of all others, the command of the army, which they sent afterwards to Italy, to reconquer the kingdom of Naples. Either by the fault of the French, or the inconstancy of their allies, this expedition failed, or, at least produced little advantage : Yet the ill success was not imputed to the Duke, who drew from it more glory than he could have done from a victory— For this reason: Philip the second King of Spain, upon the abdication of his father, Charles the Vth. turned his arms against the frontiers of France, and entered through Flanders into Picardie, to make a diversion from the war in Italy. The Constable, as Governor of that Province, was then obliged to take leave of the King, and, against his inclination, run the hazards of war. The loss of the battle of Saint-Quintin, where the Spaniards took him prisoner, spread a consternation through all the neighbouring provinces. The friends of the Guises in council, could discover no surer means of repelling this invasion of the enemy, of repairing the losses, and preventing the consequences of this defeat, than by recalling from Italy the Duke of Guise. The celerity of his return, added to the memorable conquests of Calais, Guisne, and Thionville, fully justified these hopes, and gave him that superiority over the Constable, that a Conqueror must ever have over one who is conquered.

The Constable, however, obtained his liberty, and returned to court. The King's affection for him was not abated. Henry, attributing his late misfortunes to the lot of arms, and the fortune of war, conversed familiarly with him, and, still convinced of his capacity, confided to him the weight of public affairs. In the critical circumstances

ftances of the State, the Duke and the Cardinal, who had acquired a great reputation, the one by his exploits, and the other by his abilities, apprehended that if they could not throw fome powerful obftacle in the way of the Conftable, he would rife higher in favor than ever. They refolved therefore to gain to their party, Diana, Dutchefs of Valentinois—to connect their interefts with hers—and to make her protection and favor ferve as a foundation of their elevation. And who was Diana? Of illuftrious birth, defcended from the ancient houfe of the Counts of Poitiers, in the flower of her age, fhe united with uncommon beauty, a fprightly wit, an acute and fubtle underftanding, the moft infinuating graces of behavior, and all the other qualities which in a young woman, enchant the eyes and captivate the heart. She had married the Senechal of Normandy, who foon left her a widow, with two daughters. She took advantage of her fingle ftate to deliver herfelf up to the pleafures and amufements of the Court. Her charms gained the heart of the King, whom fhe governed with an abfolute empire. But fhe behaved with fo much arrogance, and appropriated to herfelf the riches of the crown, with fo much avidity, that fhe made herfelf odious and infupportable to the whole kingdom. The Queen, full of indignation, to have a rival fo powerful, behaved towards her with an exterior decency, but in her heart bore her an implacable hatred. The nobility, whom fhe had ill treated in the perfons of feveral gentlemen, could not with patience, fee themfelves trampled under foot by the pride of a woman—and the people detefted her avarice—to which they imputed the rigorous impofts, with which they were loaded.

The

The Guifes, without regard to the general difcontent—fenfible only to the fear of lofing their power, fought the friendfhip of the Dutchefs, who foon declared herfelf openly in their favor, and by marrying one of her daughters to the Duke of Aumale, their brother, fupported them with all her credit. The Conftable eafily unravelled the intrigues of the Guifes, and, not depending on the marks of confidence which he received from the King, thought to fortify himfelf, equally, with the protection of Diana. If the Guifes had flattered her, by the fplendor of their birth, he did not defpair to gain her to his intereft, by fatiating her avarice, a paffion as ungovernable in her heart, as ambition. He began to make his court to her, and endeavored to gain her by confiderable prefents. He had fo much at heart the fuccefs of his meafures, that in fpite of his natural pride, he did not hefitate to feek alfo her alliance by efpoufing to Henry Lord of Damville, his fecond fon, Antoinette de la Mark, grand daughter by the mother, of the Dutchefs of Valentinois—a refolution fo much the more imprudent, as Diana was already ftrictly united with the party of the Guifes, and labor'd fincerely, with all her power, for their aggrandizement—whereas fhe favored but coldly the defigns of the Conftable. All the means which had been employed in oppofition to the elevation of the Guifes, became ufelefs. To the merit of their fervices—to the intrigues by which they had continually advanced themfelves ; at the time, when they difputed with fo much vivacity with their rivals, for the firft rank at the Court, was added, the marriage of Francis, the Dauphin of France, and the eldeft fon of the

N   King,

King, with the Princefs Mary, fole heir of the kingdom of Scotland, daughter of James Stuart, lately deceafed, by Mary of Lorrain, fifter of the Duke and Cardinal. An alliance of fo much magnificence, drew them near to the throne. There remained now, to the Conftable and his family, only the friendly fentiments, which the King preferved for them by habit ; and to the other courtiers, only the offices of fmaller importance. The principal dignities, the faireft governments, and the general fuperintendance of affairs, civil and military, all were placed in the hands of the Guifes and their creatures.

While all minds, were held in agitation at Court by thefe events, the Bourbons faw themfelves, notwithftanding their proximity of blood, and pretenfions to the crown, contrary to the ufage of the nation, excluded from employments and honors. Except when the neceffity of a war, or the exercife of fome office of little confequence, which remained to them, required their prefence, they appeared not at Court. It is true, that the Count D'Aguien, one of the Princes of this houfe, had advanced himfelf by his merit and valour. The King had given him the command of his army in Piedmont. The battle of Cerizolles, which he gained againft the Spaniards, had raifed his reputation. But this advantage was too tranfitory to raife the houfe of Bourbon. This Prince died by accident, in the flower of his age, and his brother, the Duke D'Anguien was killed at the battle of St. Quintin. There remained therefore none of the children of Charles of Bourbon, but Anthony Duke of Vendome, and King of Navarre, by his marriage with Jane of Albret ; Louis, Prince of Conde, the ftock of the

the branches of Condé and Conti, killed afterwards at Jarnac, and Charles, Cardinal of Bourbon, proclaimed King afterwards by the Leaguers, under the name of Charles the tenth.

The chiefs of the house, were now, Anthony Duke of Vendome, and Louis Prince of Condé, his brother, both sons of Charles of Vendome, who, after the revolt of the Constable de Bourbon, and the captivity of Francis the first, by his moderation and disinterestedness, had somewhat calmed the hatred which had been violently enkindled against those of his blood. These Princes, depressed by the Guises, whom they called strangers and new comers from Lorrain, complained bitterly, that except the right of succession to the crown, which no man could take from them, they were deprived of all their privileges, and especially of the honor of residing near the person of the King. That they scarcely held any rank in a court, where their birth called them to the first places after his Majesty : and that such conduct was equally inconsistent with reason and equity. The King, however, maintained with inflexibility, the power of the Guises against all remonstrances and complaints. The Bourbons endured with less impatience, the elevation of the Constable Montmorency : on the contrary, they were severely mortified to see his credit diminish. United with him by an alliance, by views and by interests, they flattered themselves they might obtain by his means a decent rank, if they could not re-ascend to that which their ancestors had possessed. But now, deprived of that hope which supports the unfortunate, by softening the sentiment of their ills, they bore with still greater impatience their disgraces.

Anthony

Anthony of Vendome, a Prince of a mild and moderate character, appeared to support them with more tranquility than the others, becaufe he meditated great defigns. He had married Jane of Albret, only daughter of Henry, King of Navarre, and after the death of his father in law he had taken the crown and title of King. His project was to recover his kingdom of Navarre, of which the Spaniards had made themfelves mafters, for feveral years, during the war between Louis the XIIth, and Ferdinand the Catholic. The Kings of France, to whofe intereft this ftate had been facrificed, had attempted feveral times to reconquer it. The Spaniards, who could eafily march troops to its relief, had hitherto defended it. But the two crowns, being then upon the point of concluding a folid peace, the King of Navarre, hoped to comprehend in the treaty, and to obtain a reftitution of his hereditary ftates, or, at leaft, an equivalent. He was confirmed in this thought, by the birth of a fon, to whom he gave the name of Henry, in memory of his maternal grandfather. This is the Prince, whom, the fplendor of his victories raifed, after long and bloody wars, to the throne of France, under the name of Henry the fourth, and whofe exploits and virtues have merited the name of great. He was born the 13th of December, 1554, at Pau, the capital of Bern. This birth, which filled with joy the King and Queen of Navarre, infpired them with more ardor, to recover their dominion. Anthony chofe rather to intereft the King of France, to demand this reftitution in the treaty of peace, than to folicit in quality of firft Prince of the blood, governments and dignities in the kingdom. It was this,

this, which engaged him to diffemble with more
patience and moderation than the reft, the injuftice done to his houfe. The King, perfifting
in the defign of lowering continually the Princes
of the blood, or perhaps irritated at the refufal
of Anthony, to exchange Bearn and his other
ftates, for cities and territories fituated in the in-
terior of the kingdom, had difmembered from
Guienne, of which the King of Navarre was governor, as firft Prince of the blood, Languedoc
and the city of Touloufe, to give the government
of it, to the Conftable. But the King of Navarre,
fhewing little refentment of this injuftice, purfued conftantly his firft views.

Louis, Prince of Conde, brother to the King
of Navarre, full of ambition and inquietude,
and not reftrained by fimilar interefts, faw with
grief the mediocrity of his fortune, anfwer fo ill
to the fplendor of his birth. Without offices,
governments, or employments to fupport him,
he could not bear, but with a difcontent which
he took no pains to conceal, the exceffive grandeur of the Guifes, who monopolized for themfelves the firft dignities and faireft employments
of the kingdom. To his perfonal mortification
he joined the difgrace of the Conftable, whofe
niece he had efpoufed. He was fo ftrictly connected with him, and the Marchal of Montmorency his fon, that he faw in the humiliation of their
houfe, the completion of his own misfortunes.
The Admiral of Chatillon, and D'Endelot, his
brother, irritated him ftill more by their advice.
The firft was an ambitious, but an able politician,
who took a fecret advantage of all occafions, to
profit of troubles to raife himfelf to high power.
The other, fiery, paffionate, continually occupied

in

in intrigues and plots, ceafed not, by his difcourfe and example to nourifh in the heart of Louis, the hatred already too deeply inkindled. This Prince, tranfported with rage, and almoft reduced to defpair, faw no refource for him, but by caufing a revolution in the State.

Such was the fituation of affairs—fuch the jealoufies and animofites of the Grandees, ready, on the flighteft occafion, to break out, in an open rupture, when, in the month of July 1559, happened the unexpected death of Henry IId. killed by accident in a tournament by Gabriel Count of Montmorency, one of the Captains of his guards.

Francis IId. his eldeft fon, with a weak underftanding, and a delicate conftitution, fucceeded him. Thofe evils, which even under his father had been expected, haftened to make themfelves felt, under his feeble reign. Secret enmities were eafily changed into declared hatreds—and recourfe was foon had to arms. The youth and imbecility of the King rendered him incapable of governing. It was neceffary that he fhould have; not a guardian, becaufe he had paffed the age of fourteen years, the term fixed for the majority of the Kings of France; but Minifters, prudent and laborious, who fhould govern under his authority, until time fhould have fortified his underftanding, and invigorated his conftitution. The ancient ufage of the kingdom, called the Princes of the blood to this place—and indicated the King of Navarre, and the Prince de Conde, who united to the proximity of blood, an eftablifhed reputation. The Duke of Guife and the Cardinal of Lorrain, uncles of the King, by his marriage with the Queen of Scots, pretended that
this

this honor belonged to them, in consideration of their long labors and services to the crown, but especially becaufe they had in fact enjoyed it, during the life of the late King. Catherine of Medicis, mother of the King, expected to govern alone : She depended on the filial tenderness of her fon— feveral examples authorised her preten-fions—but fhe founded her ftrengeft hopes on the divifions of the Grandees—and the terror of each faction, leaft the other fhould carry the point, facilitated her defign.

The Guifes were fenfible that they wanted the advantage of being of the blood, to which the laws and cuftoms of the nation had ufually confided the government of the kingdom. They forefaw moreover the empire which the councils of a mother would have over the mind of her fon, ftill young and without experience. They refolved therefore, by joining and acting in concert with her, to divide a power which they defpaired of obtaining entire. The Queen, a Princefs of refined genius and mafculine courage, knew that the Princes of the blood, fuffered with impatience the authority and grandeur of Queens. She thought alfo, that as a ftranger and an Italian fhe had occafion to fortify herfelf, with the fupport of fome faction. She confented therefore cheerfully to combine with the Guifes, whom fhe faw difpofed to accept of part of that authority, which the Bourbons would have pretended to appropriate to themfelves without partition. There was but one obftacle to the intimacy of this Union, and that was the unlucky connection of the Guifes with the Dutchefs of Valentinois, who had poffeffed the heart of the late King, to the time of his death. The occafion was prefling,

and

and the importance of the bufinefs would not admit of delay. On one hand the Queen, to whom diffimulation was not difficult, agreed to *appear*, to forget the paft, with the fame moderation which fhe had fhewn, in bearing with her rival during the life of her husband : On the other, the Guifes occupied wholly with their prefent intereft, eafily betrayed their friend, by confenting that the Dutchefs fhould be difgraced and difmiffed from the Court. They only required that fhe fhould not be totally ftripped of thofe immenfe riches, which muft one day revert to the Duke of Aumale, their brother.

The King of Navarre, was then abfent, and very difcontented with the King and the Court, who, in the treaty concluded with Spain, had given no attention to his interefts, nor to the reftitution of his States. The new coalition at Court, had, with great addrefs, diffembarraffed themfelves of the Conftable, by deputing him to do the honors of the obfequies of Henry the fecond. The perfonage who has that commiffion, muft not abfent himfelf from the place where the body is depofited, during the three and thirty days that the funeral pomp continues. Artifice and accident, having thus removed the two great obftacles, it was not difficult to obtain, of Francis the fecond, feduced by the careffes and the charms of his Scottifh Queen, an arrangement by which he placed the reins of government, in the hands of his neareft relations. Every thing which concerned the war, was committed to the Duke of Guife. The Cardinal had the departments of Juftice and Finance—and the Queen mother the fuperintendance of all parts of the government. To eftablifh their meafures, which

had

had fo well fucceeded, and that the complaints and intrigues of the difaffected might not fhake the refolution of the King, and difarrange their plan, there was no doubt but the firft ftroke of their policy would fall upon the Conftable, whofe prudence and credit were dreaded by the Guifes, and againft whom the Queen had for fome time entertained a fecret averfion. The Guifes feared him, on account of the jealoufy, which for a long time had openly divided their houfes— becaufe, notwithftanding the fall of his favour at court, the reputation of his wifdom, preferved him a great influence throughout the whole kingdom. In their fecret interviews with the King, they artfully drew the converfation to this fubject, and exaggerated to him the reputation which the Conftable enjoyed.

No. 17.

Ses mains, autour du trône, avec confufion,
Semaient la jaloufie, et la divifion.

THE Guifes, in their fecret converfations with the King, infinuated, that if the Conftable refided at the Court, he would be affuming; would think to govern his Majefty like an infant, and even to hold him under the ferule and the rod. They reprefented his intimate connections with the Bourbons, the eternal enemies of a crown, to which they had however long afpired. Finally, they fuggefted, that he could not confide in the

o   Conftable,

Conſtable, without expoſing his life, and the lives of his brothers, to the diſcretion of people, whoſe ambition the Kings, his predeceſſors, had always dreaded ; and whom they had ever held in a ſtate of humiliation, and at a diſtance from Court. Penetrating genius eaſily inſpires ſuſpicions into contracted minds. Nothing more was wanting to perſuade a weak King, to ſeek a pretext, honourably to diſmiſs the Conſtable. As ſoon as the ceremony of the obſequies of Henry IId. was compleated, the King overwhelming him with careſſes, ſignified to him, that not being able, with ſufficient dignity to acknowledge his merit, nor the value of the ſervices which he had rendered the Kings, his anceſtors, he had, reſolved to diſcharge him from the cares and burthens of government, too diſproportionate to his great age ; that he would no longer require of him, any exceſſive application to buſineſs, but would reſerve him for ſome occaſions of eclat ; that he ſhould always conſider him, not as a ſervant and a ſubject, but as a venerable father ; and that he would give him leave to retire, wherever he ſaw fit. The Conſtable eaſily comprehended that this leſſon had been taught the King, by the Guiſes, through the Queen mother, and the Queen of Scots : that it would be uſeleſs to remonſtrate ; and that it was better to receive as a recompenſe, orders, which his reſiſtance might convert into diſgrace. He thanked the King ; recommended to him his ſons and his nephews, and retired to his caſtle at Chantilly, ten leagues from Paris, where, he had more than once before, ſupported viciſſitudes of fortune.

As ſoon as the Queen mother and the Guiſes, had baniſhed the Conſtable, they ſtudied to diſembarraſs embarrafs themfelves of the Prince de Condé. It was eafy to forefee, that his fiery temper, and animofity againft the Guifes, would tranf-port him to attempt all the means imaginable, *to change the form of government eftablifhed.*

It may be remarked in this place, that thefe ex-preffions intimate an idea of reformation of gov-ernment, and regeneration of nations, like thofe which prevail at this time, in France, and in many other countries after the example of A-merica. One would conjecture that the Prince of Condé, had it in contemplation to eftablifh committees of correfpondence, to call a conven-tion, or national affembly ; to deliberate on a ra-tional plan of government, to be adopted by the nation at large. There are, indeed, in hiftory, fome traces of a party, who wifhed for a republi-can government, about this time : but unfortu-nately, their ideas of a republic, appear to have been the fame, with thofe which prevail too much at prefent, in France. Two hundred and fifty years of experience, have not yet brought the nation to advert to the true principles in nature, upon which government is founded. The Mar-quis of Condorcet, the friend of Turgot and Rochefoucault, fo great in geometry, is not more accurate in the fcience of government, than Eti-enne de la Boetie, the friend of De Thou and Montaine. The fame reformation is wanting now, that was fo neceffary in 1550. Whether a fovereignty in one fingle affembly, conftituted by a double reprefentation, as the prefent affem-bly is, would have anfwered then, or will fucceed now, are queftions that hereafter may deferve confideration. It ended formerly, after an hun-dred years of civil wars, in the fimple abfolute monarchy

monarchy of Louis XIVth. Time muſt determine whether the continued deliberations and exertions of the National Aſſembly, will finally obtain a balance in their government. This is the point, on which their ſuccefs will turn ; if they fail in this, ſimple monarchy, or what is more to be dreaded, ſimple deſpotiſm, after long ſtruggles will infallibly return. If the wild idea of annihilating the nobility ſhould ſpread far, and be long perſiſted in, the men of letters and the National Aſſembly, as democratical as they may think themſelves, will find no barrier againſt deſpotiſm. The French, as well as the Creek Indians, at this time our reſpectable gueſts, and all other nations, civilized and uncivilized, have their beloved families, and nothing but deſpotiſm ever did or ever can prevent them from being *diſtinguiſhed by the people* Theſe beloved families in France are the nobility. Five eighths of the preſent National Aſſembly are noble. The firſt freſh election will ſhow the world the attachment of the people to thoſe families.* In ſhort, the whole power of the nation will fall into their hands, and a commoner will ſtand no chance for an election after a little time, unleſs he enliſt himſelf under the banner and into the regiment of ſome nobleman. For the commoners, this project of one aſſembly is the moſt impolitic imaginable. It is the higheſt flight of ariſtocracy. To the royal authority it is equally fatal as to the commons. In what manner the nobility ought to be reformed, modified, methodized, and wrought by repreſentation or otherwiſe, into an independent branch of the legiſlature ? What form of government would have been beſt for France, under Francis IId. and whether the ſame is not

now

---

* They never dared to truſt an Election.

now neceffary, under Louis XVIth, are queftions too deep and extenfive, perhaps for us to determine. But we are very competent to demonftrate two propofitions, firft, that a fovereignty in a fingle affembly, cannot fecure the peace, liberty or fafety of the people. Secondly, that a federative republic, or in other words, a confederation of the republic of Paris, with the republics of the provinces, will not be fufficient to fecure the tranquility, liberty, property or lives of the nation. In fome future time, if neither bufinefs of more importance, nor amufements more agreeable fhould engage us, we may throw together a few thoughts, upon thefe queftions. This may be done without the fmalleft apprehenfion of ever being confuted : for altho we fhould fail to produce arguments to convince our readers, we know with infallible certainty, that time will fupply all our defects, and demonftrate for us, the truth of both the propofitions.

At prefent we return to the narration of Davila. The Prince de Condé's quality of Prince of the blood, and the want of plaufible pretexts, did not permit the Guifes, fo eafily to difmifs him from court. They found, however, a favorable occafion to fend him off, for a time, till the new Miniftry fhould be well eftablifhed, by nominating him Plenipotentiary, to the King of Spain, to ratify the peace and alliance contracted a little before the death of Henry IId. He quitted the court upon this embaffy, and left the field open for the perfection of projects, which were as yet only in fketches. The Queen mother and the Guifes proceeded in the fame manner with all whom they feared : Strongly determined to confummate their defigns, they judged that they could

could not fucceed, but by arranging all the ftrong places, as well as the troops, the finances, and all the refources of the ftate, under their own difpofition; fo that the moft important affairs fhould pafs through no hands but their own, and thofe of their creatures. Neverthelefs, to fhow that they confulted their intereft lefs than the public good and their own glory, they did not elevate to dignities, people without merit, and drawn from the duft, for fear they fhould be thought to make creatures for themfelves at any rate: but they conferred favors only on perfons, who added acknowledged merit to confpicuous birth, and above all, eftimable in the eyes of the people for integrity. This conduct had a double advantage, the firft, that the people commonly applauded their choice, and their opponents had no pretence to condemn it: the fecond, that confiding in perfons of honor and fidelity, they were not expofed to be deceived, nor to fufpect their attachment, as it often happens to thofe who commit the execution of their defigns to people of bafe extraction, or difhonored by their manners. In this view, they reftored to office, Francis Olivier, formerly chancellor of the kingdom, a perfonage of known integrity and inflexible firmnefs, in the exercife of his employment. The vigor with which he avowed and fupported his fentiments, had caufed his difmiffion from court, from the beginning of the reign of Henry IId. and the inftigations of the Conftable had not a little contributed to his difgrace. They recalled alfo to council, and near the perfon of the King, the Cardinal de Tournon, who, in the time of Francis Ift. grand-father of the reigning Prince, had the principal conduct of affairs.

affairs. By thefe meafures they flattered the
multitude, and fulfilled the expectations of the
public, without neglecting their own interefts.

The probity of the Cardinal and the Chancellor,
had rendered them dear to the people, who knew
how often they had declared themfelves againft
the multiplication of impofts, with which they
were oppreffed. Moreover, difgraced by the intrigues of the Conftable, and recalled with honor
by the Guifes, they muft, both from refentment
and gratitude, fupport with their counfels, and
all their influence, the projects of aggrandizement,
formed by the latter. Many others had been
gained by fimilar artifices : but the fame management was not ufed with the houfe of Bourbon,
nor with the family of the Conftable. On the
contrary, the Princes of Lorrain, drawn away by
the defire of annihilating the credit of their ancient rival, and of abafing the royal family, feized
with ardor, every occafion of diminifhing the
authority and increafing the loffes of their enemies.

The Admiral Gafpard de Coligni, had two
different governments ; that of the Ifle of France,
and that of Picardie ; but as the laws of the
kingdom, permitted not the poffeffion of more
than one dignity, or one government at the fame
time, the late King had deftined that of Picardie,
to the Prince de Condé, to appeafe his refentment
and foften his complaints. The Prince earneftly
defired this favor, to which, indeed, he had juft
pretenfions. His father, and the King of Navarre
had fucceffively held it ; and the Admiral had
refigned it, in confideration of the Prince. But
the death of Henry IId. happening near the fame
time, had hindered the effect of this arrangement,
which had already been made public. Francis
                                                    the

the IId. had no regard to it. At the folicitation of the Guifes, and by a manifeft injuftice to the Prince, he granted this place to Charles de Coffé, Marechal de Briffac, a captain of high reputation and great valor ; but who having been promoted by the favor of the Princes of Lorrain, was clofe-ly attached to them and ferved them with zeal. Nor was there more attention paid to Francis of Montmorency, the eldeft fon of the Conftable. He had married Diana, natural daughter of Henry IId. In confideration of this marriage, he had been promifed, the office of grand mafter of the King's houfehold, a place which had been long held by his father. From the firft days of the reign of Francis IId. the Duke of Guife, took it for himfelf, that he might add this new eclat to his other dignities, as well as deprive of it, an houfe which he wifhed to deprefs. Thus the Duke and the Cardinal, embraced with ardor, every occafion of mortifying their rivals, and aggrandizing themfelves. The Queen mother, who forefaw that this unlimited ambition and this violent hatred, muft have fatal effects, defired that they fhould act with more moderation, man-agement and dexterity ; but fhe dared not, in the beginning, oppofe herfelf to the wills, nor traverfe the defigns of thofe, whofe influence was the principal fupport of her authority.

At this time the Bourbons, excluded from all parts of the government, banifhed from court, and without hopes of carrying their complaints to the foot of the throne, beginning to reflect upon the fituation of their affairs, and the con-duct of their enemies, who, not content with their prefent grandeur, labored by all forts of means to perpetuate it, refolved, to remain no longer

longer inactive fpectators of their own misfortunes, but to prevent the ruin that threatened
them. To this purpofe a convention was called,
and we fhall foon fee what kind of convention it
was. Anthony, King of Navarre, after having
left in Bearn his fon, yet an infant, under the
conduct of the Queen his wife, as in an afylum,
at a diftance from that conflagration, which they
faw ready to be lighted up, in France, repaired to
Vendome, with the Prince of Condé, already returned from his embaffy: the Admiral, Dandelot, and the Cardinal of Chatillon, his brothers,
Charles Compte de la Rochefoucault, Francis
Vidame de Chartres, Antony Prince of Portien,
all relations or common friends, affembled alfo,
with feveral other noblemen attached for many
years to the houfes of Montmorency and Bourbon. The Conftable, who, altho to all appearance
wholly engaged in the delights of private life,
fecretly fet in motion all the fprings of this enterprize, had fent to this affembly at Ardres, his ancient and confidential Secretary, with inftructions
concerning the affairs to be there agitated. They
took into confideration the part which it was
neceffary to act in the prefent conjuncture of affairs. All agreed in the fame end, but opinions as
ufual, were divided concerning the means. All e-
qually felt the atrocious affronts committed againft
the Princes of the blood, for the Guifes, had not
only taken the firft places in the government, but
the fmall number of dignities which had remained
to them. They faw evidently that the defign
was nothing lefs, than to opprefs thefe Princes
and their partizans. All perceived the neceffity

P   of

of preventing fo preffing a danger, without waiting for the laft extremity. But they were not
equally agreed concerning the meafures proper
to ward it off.

No. 18.

L'un et l'autre parti cruel également,
Ainfi que dans le crime, eft dans l'aveuglement.

IN the affembly, convention, caucus, or confpiracy, at Ardres, call it by which name you
will, the prince de Condé, the Vidâme de Chartres, Dandelot and others, of a character more
irritable and violent, were of opinion, that without leaving to the Guifes the time to augment
their credit and their forces, they fhould fly to
arms as the remedy the moft expeditious and the
moft efficacious.

"In vain," faid they, "fhall we wait for the
King, of his own motion, to determine, to reftore
us the rank which is our right. This Prince,
incapable of deciding for himfelf, will never
come out of that lethargy, in which he has been
ftupified from his infancy. Governed by his
mother and the Guifes, he will never dare to re-
demand the power which he has fo blindly abandoned to them. How can the juft complaints of
the Princes of the blood, and the nobles, the beft
affectioned to the welfare of the ftate, ever reach
the

the ear of a monarch, who, even in the service of his person, is constantly surrounded with spies, stationed by his ministers, and sold to their tyranny ? What dependance can we have, on the resolutions of a Prince, to whom they will represent our requisitions under the blackest colours, and the odious appellations of revolts, conspiracies, and plots ? Can we hope that the Queen mother and the Guises will dismiss themselves, in favor of their enemies and rivals, from a part of that power which has cost them so much labor and so many artifices ? This expectation would be more chimerical than the former.   Men do not weakly abandon an authority, which they have once usurped with, so much boldness.   Whoever arrives, by slow and secret intrigues, to unlawful power, enjoys it haughtily, and preserves it at all hazards.   The power and authority of the laws, may impose on private persons ; but they give way to force, which alone decides the rights and interests of Princes.   So much reserve and timidity on our part, will only serve to augment the confidence and temerity of our enemies.   To begin by complaining, would be to found an alarm before an attack, and to advertise our competitors to put themselves on their guard.   The promptitude of execution, alone decides the success of great enterprizes.   Sloth and irresolution, debases the courage, enervates the forces, and loses the opportunity which flies so rapidly away. Let us hasten then to take arms, and overwhelm our enemies before they have time to collect themselves ; and let us not ruin our own hopes and projects, by cowardly precautions, and unseasonable delays."

The

The King of Navarre, the Admiral, the Prince of Portien and the Secretary of the Conftable, in the name of his mafter, rejected with horror, counfels fo extreme, and propofed remedies lefs violent. "Whatever proteftations we may make," they replied, "that we take arms only to deliver the King from the tyranny of ftrangers, and that we afpire not to his authority, our conduct will be ill interpreted. All good Frenchmen, religioufly attached to the perfon of the King, will fee our enterprize with indignation. Is it permited to fubjects to lay violence or conftraint on their fovereign, under any pretext or for any reafon whatever ? Do the laws of the kingdom authorize us, to force our mafter, to confide to us, any portion of his authority ? He has paffed his fourteenth year, and ought no longer to be in tutelage. Thus our pretenfions, formed only on decency, propriety and fimple equity, had better be urged with delicacy and moderation, than by ways fo violent as thofe of arms. By employing the means which prudence and addrefs may fuggeft to us, let us not defpair of gaining on the inclinations of the Queen mother. As foon as fhe can fee her fafety in our party, we fhall fee the power of the Guifes diffolve, and we fhall open to ourfelves a way, equally honorable and eafy to the execution of our defigns. The Princes of Lorrain have had, hitherto, no obftacle in their way ; perhaps when they fee a formidable oppofition arifing, they will determine to cede to us a part in the government. We will then avail ourfelves of opportunities, to fecure us againft the dangers which threaten us, and the outrages with which they overbear us. Is it not better to be
fatisfied

fatisfied with reafonable conditions, than to expose all to the inconftancy of fortune, and the hazardous decifion of arms ? Have we in France, forces to oppofe to our lawful fovereign ? What fuccour can we expect from foreign powers, who have lately renewed their alliances with the King ? To take arms at prefent, would be to precipitate the houfe of Bourbon into the deepeft misfortunes, rather than to open to us, an honorable reception into the government." This laft fentiment prevailed, and it was refolved that the King of Navarre, as the chief of the houfe, and the firft Prince of the blood, fhould repair to Court, and negotiate with the Queen mother, and endeavor to obtain fome part in the adminiftration of government, for himfelf, and for his brothers and partifans, the governments and dignities of which they had been deprived, or others equivalent.

It was forefeen, however, that the fuccefs would not be happy. The King of Navarre, intimidated by the difficulty of the enterprize, acted with a delicacy, irrefolution and complaifance, dictated by that foftnefs and moderation which formed the effence of his character. The Guifes, on the contrary, full of that confidence, which profperity infpires, prepared to repell with vigor the attempt that was made againft them. In concert with the Queen, they repeated inceffantly to the young Monarch, that his predeceffors had always mortified the Princes of the blood, as enemies to the reigning branch, againft which they never ceafed to operate, fometimes by fecret cabals, and fometimes by open force. That in the prefent circumftances, the King of Navarre and

and the Prince de Condé, feeing themfelves fo near the throne, under a King of a tender complexion, who had no children, and whofe brothers were under age, fought only to deprive him of the fupport of his mother, and his neareft relations, that they might govern him at pleafure, and hold him in dependance, as the Maires of the Palace had formerly held the Clovis's, the Chilperics, and other Princes incapable of reigning. That perhaps there was no crime at which they would hefitate, even to employing poifon, or the fword, to open a paffage for themfelves to the throne. The King, naturally timid and fufpicious, pre-occupied by thefe artificial accufations, which were coloured with fome appearance of probability, faw with an evil eye, the King of Navarre, and received him coldly. In the audiences which he granted him, always in the prefence of the Duke and the Cardinal, who never quitted him a moment, he gave him none but dry anfwers; alledging that he was of age; that he was not refponfible to any man for his actions; that he was fatisfied with the good fervices of thofe who governed under him; and rejected conftantly all the requefts and demands of the Princes of the blood, as irregular, unreafonable, and made with ill defigns.

The efforts of the King of Navarre had no better fuccefs with the Queen-mother. She knew that fhe could not depend upon the attachment which the Princes of the blood profeffed to her; that as foon as they fhould obtain what they folicited, they would exclude her from the government, and force her perhaps to quit the Court. She judged moreover, that it would be imprudent

dent to abandon the party the moſt powerful
and the beſt eſtabliſhed, to attach herſelf to the
Princes of the blood, who had no certain ſup-
port. She determined therefore to purſue her
firſt plan : but as ſhe wiſhed to prevent the horrors of a civil war, ſhe propoſed to herſelf, not
entirely to take away all hopes from the Princes,
but to make uſe of artifice and diſſimulation, to
divert the King of Navarre, whoſe docility ſhe
knew, from the deſigns which he had formed,
and to wait, from time and conjunctures, ſome
expedient, advantageous to the welfare of the
ſtate. In conſequence, ſhe received him with
great demonſtrations of friendſhip, and amuſed
him with the faireſt hopes. In the courſe of
converſations which they had together, ſhe in-
ſinuated, that the paſſions of the King were eaſily
irritable ; that he muſt not be vexed with demands and complaints out of ſeaſon ; that it was
neceſſary to wait for opportunities more favorable ; that the King having paſſed his fourteenth
year, might govern by himſelf, and without
taking counſel of any one ; that when he ſhould
find an opportunity to manifeſt his benevolence
for the Princes of Bourbon, he would fulfil all
that was required of him, by the relations of
blood, and would prove to all the world the
eſteem and conſideration, which he entertained
of their merit and fidelity : that to change, all at
once, in the beginning of a reign, the order eſtabliſhed in the government, would be to give the
King among his own ſubjects, the reputation of
an inconſtant Prince, without prudence and without firmneſs : that if any employment worthy
of them ſhould be vacant, he would have a regard

gard to the juftice of their pretenfions : that in her own particular, fhe offered herfelf voluntarily to manage their interefts with her fon, to engage him to grant them, as foon as fhould be poffible, the fatisfaction they defired : that it was not decent that the King of Navarre, who had always evinced his wifdom and moderation, fhould now fuffer himfelf to be guided by counfels, and drawn into rafh meafures which were neither confiftent with his age nor character ; but by waiting with patience, for what depended wholly on the benevolence and affection of the King, he ought to teach others, how to merit in their due feafons, the favor and beneficence of his Majefty. The Queen having founded him, at feveral times, by fuch general difcourfes, and perceiving that he began to waver, compleatly gained him at length, by faying that they muft immediately fend into Spain, Elizabeth, the fifter of the King, who muft be attended by fome Prince, diftinguifhed by his reputation and by his rank; that fhe had caft her eyes on him, as the perfonage the moft proper to fupport the honor of the nation, by the fplendor of his virtues, and of the Majefty Royal, with which he was adorned ; that befides the fatisfaction which the King her fon would have in it, he would find a great advantage for his private pretenfions, by the facility which he would have, of conciliating the affections of the Catholic King, and at the fame time of treating in perfon of the reftitution, or of the change of Navarre. Finally, fhe promifed him to employ all her credit, and all the power of the King her fon, to infure the fuccefs of this negotiation.

The

The King of Navarre, in examining the difpofitions of the Court, had obferved that all thofe who were employed by the government, fatisfied with the prefent fituation of affairs, troubled themfelves very little about the pretenfions of the Princes of the blood—and that thofe who had an intereft to defire his grandeur, and that of his brother, either intimidated by the power of their enemies, or difconcerted by his extreme delays, defpaired equally of the fuccefs of his enterprize. He returned therefore eafily to his firft defign of recovering his ftates, and judged that he ought not to let flip an opportunity fo favourable for renewing the negotiations of accommodation with the crown of Spain, and of quitting decently a court, where he could no longer remain with honor. He accepted chearfully the commiffion of conducting the young Queen into Spain. The Queen-mother continued to delude him with magnificent hopes, and in fpight of the difcontent of the other Princes of his party, he preffed his departure with as much ardor, as even his enemies could have defired. He fuffered himfelf to be duped in Spain with the fame facility. The Queen mother had already informed Philip the fecond, of all this manœuvre. This Monarch who defired, equally with her, to fee humiliated and excluded from the government, the King of Navarre, fo ardent to make good his pretenfions to fome part of his dominions, inftructed the duke of Alva, and the other grandees who were to receive the Queen his confort, not to reject the propofitions of this Prince, but to lead him on and amufe him, by receiving them ferioufly, and offering to make report of them to his Catholic Majefty, and the council of Spain, without whofe advice they could not de-

Q   termine

termine any affair of ftate.   As foon as the King
of Navarre was arrived on the frontiers, and
had prefented the Queen Elizabeth to the Spanifh
Lords, he began to fpeak to them of his interefts,
and thought himfelf fure at firft of fuccefs.   The
Spaniards conducted the negotiation, with an addrefs which ferved to nourifh his hopes, at the
fame time that they let him know that the effect
could not be immediate.   They engaged him
even to fend ambaffadors to Madrid, fo that folely occupied with his firft defigns, he retired to
Bearn, fully refolved not to meddle in the affairs
of France, whofe negotiation appeared ineffectual,
and the project of arms as dangerous as they
were difhonorable.

The Prince of Condé his brother, had oppofite
views, and took very different refolutions.   His
fortune was not commenfurate with his courage,
nor with the extent of his defigns.   Excited by
the mediocrity of his circumftances, by the hatred which he bore to the Guifes, and inceffantly
ftimulated by his mother-in-law and his wife,
one the fifter and the other the niece of the Conftable, both devoured by ambition, he openly
detefted the government of the Queen-mother
and the Guifes.   All his thoughts and actions
tended to a revolution.   He figured to himfelf,
that if the war fhould be enkindled by his intrigues and for his interefts, not only he would
become the chief of a numerous party, but moreover he would procure to himfelf riches, advantages, and perhaps the fovereignty of feveral
cities and provinces of the Kingdom.   Full of
thefe high ideas he affembled again at La Ferte,
an eftate of his inheritance, fituated on the frontiers of Champaine, the Princes of his blood, and
the principal lords of his party, and harrangued
them

them in this manner. " In vain, have we hitherto employed the means of delicacy and moderation. It is not hereafter but by the moft vigorous efforts that we can prevent the ruin of the
royal family, and of all thofe who have not been
able to refoive to cringe fervilely under the tyranny of the Queen-mother and the Guifes. It
is no longer feafonable to diffemble outrages of
waich no man can be ignorant and which we
have fuffered with too much patience. We are
banifhed from court, and the government of Picardy, and the office of grand-mafter is taken
from us. Finances, offices, dignities, are the
prey of foreigners and perfons unknown, who
hold the King in captivity. The truth never
reaches the throne. The beft part of the nation
is oppreffed to elevate traitors, who fatten on the
blood of the people, and the treafures of the ftate.
It is on violence that the tyranny of thefe ftrangers, is founded, who perfecute with fo much
ferocity the royal blood : let us employ violence
alfo to deftroy this tyranny. It will not be the
firft time that the Princes of the blood, fhall have
taken arms to maintain their rights. Peter,
Duke of Brittany, Robert, Earl of Dreux, and
feveral other Lords oppofed, during the minority
of Saint Louis, the Queen Blanche his mother,
who had feized on the government. Philip, Earl
of Valois, employed all his forces, to exclude
from the regency, thofe who pretended to ufurp
it. Under Charles the VIIIth, Louis, Duke of
Orleans, took arms to caufe himfelf to be elected
regent, inftead of Ann, Duchefs of Bourbon, who,
in quality of eldeft fifter of the young King, had
taken into her hands the reins of the ftate. Let
us imitate our wife anceftors, let us follow fuch
ftriking examples. We find ourfelves in the
fame

fame cafe : it is therefore our duty to employ the fame means to fave the nation. Let not the apparent pleafure of the King reftrain us. This Prince, buried in a lethargic dream, and in his own imbecility, perceives not the deplorable flavery to which they have reduced him. He waits, from the Princes of the blood, the affiftance, which is expected from an enlightened and fkilful phyfician, by patients who feel not their diftempers and know not their danger. The duties of our birth, and the unanimous wifhes of the nation, authorize us to break the fetters with which this Prince is loaded, and to redrefs the evil before it arrives at its laft extremity. A vigorous refolution muft be taken without delay. Let us haften to be beforehand with our enemies, if we wifh to furmount a thoufand obftacles, which will arreft us, if we wafte the time in deliberation, and which a fudden execution alone can overcome, floth and timidity will only aggravate upon our necks the weight of a yoke equally fhameful and fatal. Can we hefitate when our tranquility, our honor and our lives have no other refource, than in the valor of our arms ?''

This difcourfe pronounced with a military tone, had already agitated minds before difpofed to take arms, both from attachment to his houfe, and their private interefts. But the Admiral, Coligni, who weighed more maturely all the confequences of fuch an enterprize, alone ventured to oppofe the opinion of the Prince, by advifing to employ in the execution of his defign, a mean more proper to enfure the fuccefs of it. "It would be," faid Coligni, "too defperate a refolution to expofe fo openly to the hazards of war, the fortunes of the houfe of Bourbon, and of fo great a number of perfons allied to their
blood,

blood, or attached to their interefts. We are not fupported by any forces at home, or alliances abroad We have no fortified places, and are without troops, and without money. In the impoffibility to act with open force, let us fub-ftitute policy in the ftead of force. Let us en-deavor, without difcovering ourfelves, to employ other arms, to execute for us, what we are not in a condition to undertake for ourfelves. The kingdom is filled with a multitude of people, who have embraced the doctrine lately introduced by Calvin. The feverity of the refearches made for them, and the rigour of their punifhments, reduce them to defpair, and to the defire as well as neceffity of braving every danger to refcue themfelves from a deftiny fo horrible. They all know, that the duke of Guife, and efpecially the Cardinal of Lorrain, are the principal authors of the perfecution ; that this laft purfues ardently their deftruction, in the Parliaments and in the King's councils, and never ceafes to rail at their doctrines, in his public harrangues and private converfations. If the difcontents of this multi-tude have not blazed out, it has been merely for want of a leader capable of guiding it, and of ani-mating it, by his example. If they fhould be fti-mulated ever fo little, they will blindly confront the greateft dangers, in the hope of delivering themfelves from the misfortunes which threaten them. Let us avail ourfelves of this refource ; let us encourage this multitude, already difpofed to commotions; let us give a form to their de-figns ; let us arm their hatred againft the Guifes ; let us put them in a condition to attack thefe ftrangers, in good order and with advantage. Our defigns, in this way, will execute themfelves, without expofing or committing us, without our
appearing

appearing to have any part in them. In augmenting our forces with all thofe of the Calvinifts, we fhall fupport ourfelves by the protection of the Proteftant Princes of Germany, and of Elizabeth Queen of England, who patronize openly the new religion. Our caufe will become better and our pretext more plaufible. We will reject upon the Proteftants the boldnefs of their enterprize. and we fhall convince the whole world, that it is neither intereft nor ambition, but fimply the difference in religion which has excited us to arms."

It fhould be remembered here, that Davila was a Catholic, and Coligni a Proteftant. The latter, one of the greateft, altho the moft unfortunate men of his age, was as fincere in religion, as pure in morals, and as honourable in the whole conduct of his life, as any one of his contemporaries. That he was defirous of engaging the Bourbons and Montmorencies to favor the alvinifts and liberty of confcience, is probable : but he is reprefented by the beft French Hiftorians, as fo much attached to the King, as to have been even fufpected by his party. The harrangue which Davila puts into his mouth, is too much like a mere politician, and too little like a philofopher or a chriftian, to be confiftent with his character.
                                     No.

No. 19.

Mais l'un et l'autre Guife ont eu moins de fcrupule.
Ces chefs ambitieux d'un peuple trop credule,
Couvrant leurs intérêts de l intérêt des cieux
Ont conduit dans le piége un peuple furieux.

THE eloquence and authority of Coligni, prevailed with the others to embrace the party of the Calvinifts, to whofe doctrines, were fecretly devoted feveral of the noblemen then prefent in the affembly. The common voice was in favor of this advice, which affording hopes, as near accomplifhment, and beeter founded, diverted them from taking arms of a fudden, and concealed for fometime, the view of dangers, to which the moft determined do not expofe themfelves, but in the laft extremity.

After Martin Luther had introduced into Germany, the liberty of thinking in matters of religion, and erected the ftandard of reformation; John Calvin, a native of Noyon, in Picardy, of a vaft genius, fingular eloquence, various erudition, and polifhed tafte, embraced the caufe of reformation. In the books which he publifhed, and in the difcourfes which he held, in the feveral cities of France, he propofed one hundred and twenty eight articles, in oppofition to the Creed of the Roman Catholic Church. Thefe opinions were foon embraced with ardor and maintained with obftinacy, by a great number of perfons of all conditions. The afylum and the centre of this new fect, was Geneva, a city fituated on the lake anciently called Lamanus, on the frontiers of Savoy, which had fhaken off the yoke of its Bifhops and the Dukes of Savoy, and erected itfelf

felf into a republic, under the title of a free city, for the fake of liberty of confcience. From this city proceeded printed books, and men diftinguifhed for their wit and eloquence, who fpreading themfelves in the neighbouring provinces, there fowed in fecret the feeds of their doctrine. Almoft all the cities and provinces of France began to be enlightened by it. It began to introduce itfelf into the kingdom, under Francis Ift. in oppofition to all the vigorous refolutions which he took to fupprefs it. Henry IId. ordained, with inexorable feverity, the punifhment of death againft all who fhould be convicted of Calvinifm. The Cardinal of Lorrain, was the high prieft, and the proud tyrant, who counfelled and ftimulated the King, to thofe cruelties and perfecutions, which, by the fhedding the blood of all the advocates of civil liberty, might have wholly fupprefled it, if the unexpected death of Henry IId. which the Calvinifts regarded as a miracle wrought in their favor, had not occafioned fome relaxation under Francis IId. The Duke of Guife and the Cardinal of Lorrain, perfifted in their bloody perfecuting refolutions : but they did not find in the Parliament nor in the other magiftrates, the fame promptitude to execute the orders which they gave in the name of the King.

Theodore Beza, a difciple of Calvin, celebrated for his eloquence and erudition, had already converted feveral perfons of both fexes, and of the firft nobility of the kingdom : and it was no longer in the ftables and cellars that the Calvinifts held their affemblies, and preached their fermons, but in the houfes of gentlemen, and in the palaces of the great. The people called them Huguenots, or Aignoffen Confederates. The Admiral Coligni and feveral other noblemen, had indeed embraced
the

the new doctrine as it was called : but the Calvinifts, reftrained by the fear of punifhment, ftill
held their affemblies in fecret, and the great dared
not declare openly for them.

The Bourbons, finding France in a condition
fo favorable to their prefent interefts, embraced
greedily the propofition of Coligni, and they de-
puted Dandelot and the Vidâme de Chartres to
negotiate this affair with the Calvinifts. Thefe
able agents, who had both embraced Calvinifm,
eafily found a multitude of perfons difpofed to
communicate to others the project in contemplation, and to make the neceffary preparations for
its execution. The Calvinifts agitated without
interruption by the terror of dangers and punifhments, ferved them with fo much promptitude
and concert, that they placed things in a train,
in a fhort time to fucceed.

The firft meafure advifed by Dandelot and the
Vidâme de Chartres, was that a large number of
thofe who profeffed the Proteftant religion, fhould
affemble and prefent themfelves without arms at
court, to petition the King for liberty of confcience, the public exercife of their religion, and
permiffion to have temples for that purpofe.
Davila, the Catholic and Italian, has recorded in
this place, all the party exaggerations of his miftrefs
and the Guifes. He fays, that if the petition of
the Proteftants was feverely and haughtily rejected, as it indubitably would be, they were to
march immediately troops affembled fecretly
from all the Provinces ; that thefe fhould fuddenly appear under different leaders who fhould be
appointed for them, that finding the King un-

R   guarded

guarded and the court without defence, they were to maffacre the duke of Guife and the Cardinal of Lorrain, with all their creatures ; and oblige the King to declare, regent and lieutenant-general of the kingdom, the Prince of Condé, who fhould grant them a ceffation of punifhment and liberty of confcience. It was believed at the time and publifhed, that the chiefs of the confpiracy, had given fecret orders, if every thing fucceeded to their wifhes, to put to the fword the Queen-mother, the King himfelf, and his brothers, that the crown in this way might defcend to the Princes of Bourbon. But Davila himfelf acquits them of this attrocious accufation, by adding, that none of the accomplices having avowed this horrible defign, neither when on the rack, nor of their own accord, but all on the contrary having formally denied it, I cannot relate it as a fact. We know very well that fame, aided by the vain terrors of the people, and the malignity of the great, takes a pleafure in magnifying objects to infinity.

The plan being thus concerted among the confpirators, they divided the provinces and employments, among the principal Calvinifts, that the execution might be attended with as much order and fecrecy as poffible. Barri, de la Renaudie affumed the principal part, and put himfelf at the head of the enterprize. This was a perfon celebrated for his travels and adventures. His wit and courage had acquired him credit among the Huguenots. He wanted neither fpirit to undertake nor vivacity to execute. The difarrangements of his fortune had reduced him to the alternative

ternative of procuring himfelf a better condition by fome daring attempt, or of terminating his misfortunes by a fudden death. Although iffued from the firft nobility of Perigord, he had wandered long in different countries, and had at length taken refuge in Geneva, where by his fubtilty he had acquired fome confideration. Such was the birth and character of the principal leader of the confpiracy, who was foon followed by a great number of affociates, fome excited by a zeal for religion, others by the attractions of novelty, and others fimply by that natural inquietude, which never permits the French to languifh in idlenefs.

La Renaudie confided to the chiefs among them, the care of affembling their partizans and conducting them to the rendezvous. The intelligence with which he diftributed provinces, introduced a kind of order into this confufion. Caftelneau had the department of Gafcony, Mazers that of Bearn, Dumefnil that of Limofin, Mirabeau that of Saintonge, Coueville, Picardy; Mourans, Provence; Maligni, Champaine; Saint-Marie, Normandy; and Montejean, Brittany : all famous for courage, diftinguifhed by their nobility, and confidered in their cities and cantons, as heads of the party. Thefe factionaries, after having affembled at Nantes, a city of Brittany, fome under the pretext of a lawfuit, and others under that of a marriage, repaired with great diligence to the pofts which were affigned them. In a few days, and with admirable fecrecy, they there gained an infinite number of perfons of all conditions, ready to facrifice their lives for an enterprize, which their preachers affured them
                                        tended

tended to the advantage and tranquility of the state.

The Prince of Condé, who secretly lighted up this conflagration, advanced by moderate days journeys to court. He wished to be witness of the event, and to take suddenly, according to circumstances, the part which should appear to him the most advantageous. The Admiral, always circumspect, feigned to remain neuter. He retired to his estate at Chatillon, under the pretext of enjoying the sweets of private life, without meddling with affairs of the public, or of government; but in reality it was as much to aid the conspiracy, by his councils and information, as to avoid the accidents which might defeat an enterprize which he judged rash and dangerous. The conspirators, who were not agitated with similar anxieties, but full of the most flattering hopes, had begun their march in secrecy, carrying their arms concealed under their cloaths. They advanced separately by different roads, and in the order which had been marked out by their chiefs, towards Blois, where the court resided at that time. This city was open on all sides, and without fortifications, and the conspirators were to meet in its suburbs, on the fifteenth day of March, 1560.

But whatever might be the activity of their proceedings and the secrecy of their councils, they could not escape the penetration of the Guises. The favors, pensions and employments they confered, and their great reputation, had attached to them so many creatures in the different provinces of the kingdom, that they were punctually informed of all the movements of the conspirators. It was indeed impossible that the march

march of fo numerous a multitude could remain unknown, when confpiracies whofe fecrets are confined to a fmall number of perfons, of the moft confummate difcretion and fidelity, are almoft always difcovered before their execution. Whether the fecret was difcovered by La Renaudie, or Avenelles, or difcovered by the fpies employed by the miniftry, even in the houfes of the principal confpirators, or whether information of it came from Germany; as foon as the Guifes had received it, they deliberated on the means of defeating it.

The Cardinal of Lorrain, who was no foldier, advifed to affemble the nobility of the neareft provinces, to draw from the neighbouring cities all the garrifons to form a body of troops, and to fend orders to all the commanders and governors to take the field, and put to the fword, all the men whom they fhould find in arms. He prefumed that the confpirators, perceiving themfelves to be difcovered, and informed of the meafures taken againft them, and which fame would not fail to exaggerate, would diffipate of themfelves. The duke of Guife, more familiar with danger, and defpifing the tranfports of a multitude, without difcipline or order, regarded the advice of the Cardinal, as more proper to palliate the diftemper, than to cure it; adding that fince it was fo pernicious, and had infinuated itfelf into the heart of the kingdom, it was ufelefs to temporize, and give it opportunity to break out with more violence. He thought it therefore, more prudent to diffemble, and affect ignorance of the enterprize, to draw in the confpirators, and give them time to difcover themfelves; that in fuch a cafe, their defeat and punifhment
would

would deliver France from a fatal contagion, which, as it difcovered itfelf by fymptoms fo terrible, demanded violent remedies, and not fimple lenitives. He added, that in punifhing feparately only a part of the confpirators, they fhould furnifh matter to the ill intentioned, to calumniate the authors of this feverity ; that the people, little accuftomed to fuch infurrections, would regard this as a chimera, and as a fable, invented by the miniftry to crufh their enemies, and eftablifh their own power and authority : whereas, by overwhelming all the confpirators at once, when upon the point of execution, they fhould diffipate all falfe accufations, and juftify in the fight of all the world, the rectitude and the fincerity of the intentions of thofe who were at the head of affairs.

Catharine agreed with the duke, No extraordinary preparation was made, which could excite a fufpicion that the confpiracy was known. They only removed the King and the court to *Amboife* ten leagues from *Blois*. This caftle, fituated on the Loire, and in the midft of forefts which fortify it, naturally, appeared to be a fafer afylum : as it was eafy to place in fecurity the King and the two Queens, in the caftle, while a fmall number of troops fhould defend the entrance of the village, which was of difficult accefs.

Eagle eyed, high foul'd ambition, feldom miffes its opportunity. The Guifes refolved to profit of a conjuncture fo advantageous to cement and increafe their power, by caufing the fall of their rivals to promote their own elevation, as poifons are fometimes, by uncommon fkill converted into remedies. They entered the King's apartments, without the knowledge of the Queen, affecting
with

with terror to exaggerate the danger; they declared all was reported to be plotted againſt the government, his moſt faithful ſubjects, and his royal perſon. They remonſtrated to him, that the danger was imminent, that the conſpirators were already at the gates of Amboiſe, with forces much more formidable and numerous than had been ſuſpected. Finally they demanded orders, the promptitude and energy of which ſhould be proportioned to the grandeur and proximity of the danger. The King, naturally timid as well as weak, and at this moment forcibly ſtricken with the greatneſs of the danger which threatened him, ordered the Queen, and all his miniſters to be called, to conſult on the means proper to repreſs the impetuoſity of ſo violent a rebellion. Nothing was ſeen on all ſides but ſubjects of terror : Every meaſure that was propoſed appeared hazardous. The Cardinal of Lorrain exhauſted all his artifices and all his eloquence to exaggerate the danger and increaſe the irreſolution. The king incapable of deciding, and of ſuſtaining the weight of government in circumſtances ſo critical, nominated, of his own mere motion, the Duke of Guiſe, his Lieutenant General, with full and compleat authority. He added, that not feeling himſelf adequate to act, he abandoned to the prudence and valor of the Duke, the conduct of his kingdom, and the care of appeaſing the troubles which agitated it.

Catharine, although ſhe felt an indignation at this bold attempt, could not oppoſe it, without an open rupture with the Guiſes, in a moment when the ſafety of the State depended on their union. She perceived the occaſion there was for

a Chief,

a Chief, whofe experience and reputation might
take place of the imbecility and irrefolution of
the king, as likely to enervate the courage of his
own troops, as to increafe the infolence of his
enemies.   Monarchs the moft abfolute, and even
republics the moft jealous of their liberty, had often conferred the fupreme authority on a fingle
man, when the greatnefs of dangers had appeared
to require a refource fo extraordinary.   Befides
thefe views, which regarded the prefervation of
her fon and his States, fhe forefaw the carnage,
which could not fail to be made, and that the
hatred of the Princes of the blood, and the enmity of the people would fall necelfarily on the
Duke of Guife commanding alone, with an abfolute authority.

The integrity of the Chancellor Olivier, was
ftill an obftacle; little fatisfied that an authority
fo unlimited fhould be granted to a fubject, he
appeared to fufpend his judgment.   His credit
and firmnefs might have prolonged, if not defeated the meafure.   The Queen-mother however
determined him, by alledging, that as foon as the
ftorm fhould be diffipated, they might reftrain by
new edicts and frefh declarations the exceffive
power to be given to the Duke, and confine him
within the bounds of duty and reafon ; that it
was the intereft of all, that the effufion of blood
fhould be done by the fole orders of the Duke,
and that neither the King, his relations, or minifters, fhould appear to dip their hands in it.
The Chancellor perfuaded by thefe reflections,
fealed the commiffion, giving to the Duke of
Guife the title and authority of Lieutenant General of the King, in all the provinces and territories of his obedience, with abfolute power, as
well in civil as military affairs.

The

The Duke as foon as he had obtained the dignity and authority which he had always defired, turned his attention to fupprefs the confpiracy. He made able and foldierlike arrangements for defending the caftle and village of Amboife, and fent out parties of cavalry as well as infantry to attack the infurgents. A detail of their fkirmifhes would be as little interefting, as it would be to the purpofe we have in view. La Renaudie fought with a bravery which well became the Proteftant caufe, and fell with Pardaillan, his antagonift, in the combat—though his foldiers collected in hafte, could not ftand againft veteran troops. A Capt. Ligniers, one of the confpirators, terrified at the greatnefs of the danger, in the moment of execution, or ftricken with remorfe, or defirous of making his court, abandoned his accomplices, and galloped by another road to Amboife. He detailed to the King and Queen, the quality and number of the confpirators, the names of their chiefs, and the roads by which they were approaching. The Prince de Condé was immediately put under guard, by order of the king, to hinder him in any manner from favoring the enterprize of the infurgents, as he promifed them. The confpirators in fine were defeated and difperfed. Some perifhed in the flames of the houfes to which they fled—others were hanged upon the trees in the neighbourhood, or on the battlements of the caftle. Multitudes were maffacred in the neighbourhood of Amboife ; the Loire was covered with dead bodies—the blood run in ftreams in the ftreet— and the public places were filled with bodies hanging on gallowffes. The punifhment of thefe miferable men, tormented by the foldiers, and

s   butchered

butchered by executioners—feverities, which the
Guifes, thought neceffary, became the fource of
carnage, and of rivers of blood, which deluged
France for many years in a moft tragical and deplorable manner.

No. 20.

Faible enfant, qui de Guife adorait les caprices,
Et dont on ignorait les vértus et les vices.

ALTHOUGH the infurgents were difperfed,
and their leaders executed, the Bourbons and the
other grandees of their party, the fecret authors
of the confpiracy, ftill lived. The council of the
King, in examining into the motives of the late
troubles, agreed without difficulty, that they
were the work of the Princes of the blood ; and
that, to maintain the authority of the King and
the Miniftry, the only fure means would be to
rid themfelves of the chiefs and authors of the
confpiracy, as perturbators of the public repofe,
as favorers of Herefy, and as rebels, who attempting the perfon of their fovereign, had violated
the fundamental laws of the monarchy. But the
Princes of the blood, were too nearly on a level
with the King; they had too much influence
with the people; they had too much power
in the ftate. The King indeed was furious,
the Queen-mother was anxious, the Guifes a-
fraid of loofing their power : But the Conftable
Montmorenci, the King of Navarre, and the
Prince

Prince de Condé, all fuppofed to be at the bottom of the evil, had fo much confequence in the world, that nothing but diffimulaiton and irrefolution prevailed in the cabinet.

The Council, after difguifing under a veil of deep diffimulation, its real defign, refolved at length, to convoke the affembly of *the States General, in whom refides the whole authority of the Kingdom.* Two reafons determined them : firft, That to execute the important refolution of the King againft the Princes of his blood, it would be ufeful to have it confirmed, by the unanimous, or at leaft the apparent confent of the nation. The fecond reafon was, that by declaring that they meant to deliberate in this affembly on the meafures neceffary to compofe the prefent troubles, to regulate the affairs of religion, and to adjuft the adminiftration of the ftate, for the future, the King would have a plaufible pretext, to fummon about his perfon, all the Princes of the blood, and all the officers of the crown, without giving them umbrage ; and that they would be inexcufable not to come, fince they were promifed, that the deliberations fhould be concerning a reformation of government, which they appeared fo much to defire. *Kings, fays Davila, never fee with pleafure, or indeed voluntarily, thefe affemblies of the States General, where their authority feems to be eclipfed, by the fovereign power of the nation, whofe deputies reprefent the whole body.*

Upon this paffage, the French writers cry out, " It is a ftranger who fpeaks, ill informed of the fundamental conftitution of our monarchy." " This Italian imagines that the royal authority was fufpended, during the feffion of the States General. But it was the royal authority which
called

called them together : without it, they could
not have affembled ; and the fame authority had
a right to difmifs them at its preafure : it is
therefore evident that their power was always
fubordinate to that of the Monarch." But this
confequence does not follow. The royal authority in England, has the power of convoking,
proroguing and diffolving Parliament : yet Parliament is not fubordinate to the royal authority,
but fuperior to it ; as the whole is fuperior to a
third part. The fovereignty is in Parliament, or
the legiflative power ; not in the King, or the
Executive. So the fovereignty might be in the
States General, comprehending the King. If
there are " twenty examples of the States General convening and feparating, by the fimple orders of the King ;" if " the Dauphin, Charles Vth,
during the detention of King John his father,
convoked feveral times the States General, and
difmiffed them when he judged proper," it will
not follow from all this, that the States were not
a part of the fovereignty : nor will it follow that
they had no authority but to advife and remon-
ftrate. " If the fentiments of the Italian author
were true," add thefe writers, " it would follow
that the authority of Parliaments and courts or
companies, whofe power is nothing but an ema-
nation from the royal authority, would be fufpended, during the feffion of the States General ;
a pretenfion abfolutely contrary to the ufages and
maxims of the kingdom." But how does it appear, that the power of the Parliaments and
courts or companies, were emanations of the
royal authority ? There is more probability that
they were originally committees of the States
General, and in that cafe their power would not
be

fufpended, unlefs it were exprefsly fufpended by a refolution or order of the ftates. But if thefe tribunals were only a part of the executive power, and conftituted by the King, it would not follow from this conceffion, that the States General were no part of the fovereignty or legiflative power. Is there one national act upon record, which acknowledges the King of France to be an unlimited fovereign? If there is not, the opinion of Davila appears to be better founded, than that of his Critick. There was always a rivalry between the royal authority and that of the States, as there is now between the power of the King and that of the National Affembly, and as there ever was, and will be in every legiflature or fovereignty which confifts of two branches only. The proper remedy then would have been the fame as it muft be now, to new model the legiflature, make it confift of three equiponderant independent branches, and make the executive power one of them; in this way, and in no other, can an equilibrium be formed, the only antidote againft rivalries. The rivalry between the Kings and States General in France, proceeded in the ftruggle for fuperiority, till the power of the former increafing and that of the latter diminifhing, the States General were laid afide after 1614, and the crown on the head of Lewis XIVth, in fact, but not of right, became abfolute: in the fame manner as the rivalry between the Popes and general councils proceeded, till the latter were difcontinued and his Holinefs became infallible: In fhort, every man, and every body of men, is and has a rival. When the ftruggle is only between two, whether individuals or bodies, it continues till one is fwallowed up, or annihilated,

ted, and the other becomes abfolute mafter. As all this is a neceffary confequence and effect of the emulation which nature has implanted in our bofoms, it is wonderful that mankind have fo long been ignorant of the remedy, when a third party for an umpire, is one fo eafy and obvious.

Francis IId, in this year, 1560, iffued a proclamation concerning the affairs of the nation, and declared that he had refolved to affemble at Fontainbleau, all the Princes and the Notables of his kingdom, in order to take their advice concerning the urgent neceffities of the ftate. He granted to all his fubjects full liberty to come there in perfon or by deputies, or to fend memorials to lay open their grievances, with promife to give them a favorable hearing, and to grant all their requefts as far as equity and reafon would permit.

The real intention of the Guifes at this time, was to take vengeance of their rivals: but to conceal this defign under the moft profound diffimulation, until a favorable moment fhould arrive, to carry it into execution. A feries of refinement in artifice, was practifed to put off their guard, the Prince de Condé, the Conftable de Montmorenci, the Admiral Coligni, and all the others of their party: at the fame time that arrangements were made in all the Provinces, and troops were affembled about the court, under commanders who were in its confidence.

About this time died the Chancellor Olivier, deftroyed, as was reported, by chagrin at the cruelties practifed at Amboife, and was fucceeded by Michel de L'Hôpital, who united to a profound erudition, a confummate experience in bufinefs. To fhow the univerfal prevalence of emulation
.and

and rivalry, of jealoufy and envy, not only between oppofite parties, but among individuals of
the fame party, it is neceffary to obferve here,
that De L'Hôpital, notwithftanding his genius,
fo penetrating and fo fruitful in refources, was
elevated, with great difficulty to this eminent
dignity by the Queen-mother, in oppofition to
the Guifes, who infifted long for Louis de Mor-
villiers. Catharine began to dread the too great
elevation of the Guifes, and wifhed to confer this
important office on a fubject entirely devoted to
her interefts.

At the affembly of the Notables at Fontainbleau, were found the chiefs of both parties, excepting the Princes of Bourbon, one of whom,
however, the King of Navarre, fent his fecretary
La Sague. After the cuftomary fpeeches of the
King, Queen, Chancellor, Duke of Guife and
Cardinal de Lorrain, Coligni arofe, approached
the King, and prefented him a paper, faying that
it was a petition of thofe of the reformed religion,
who had inftructed him to prefent it to his Majefty, founded on the faith of edicts by which he
had permitted all his fubjects to lay open their
grievances. He added, that although it was not
figned by any one, yet if his Majefty fhould order
it, one hundred and fifty thoufand men were
ready to fubfcribe it. The petition demanded
only liberty of confcience, and to have churches
for public worfhip in the cities. The Cardinal
de Lorrain, with all that impetuofity, which, the
natural vehemence of his temper added to the ardor of his fpiritual zeal and temporal ambition,
infpired, called it feditious, infolent, rafh, and
heretical : and added, that if to intimidate the
youth of the King, Coligni had advanced that it
would

would be figned by one hundred and fifty thoufand rebels, he would be refponfible for a million
of good citizens, ready to reprefs the impudence
of the factions, and compel refpect to the royal
authority.

As to the differences of religion, thofe who inclined to Calvinifm, propofed to demand of the
Pope, a free general council, where they might
difcufs and decide by common confent, the matters of controverfy : that if the Sovereign Pon-
tiff fhould refufe to grant one, the King ought,
after the example of fome of his wife predeceffors,
to affemble a national council.   But the Cardinal
of Lorrain, anfwered that there was no occafion
for any other council than that which the Pope
had already called at Trent, which had already re-
prehended and condemned the doctrines of the
innovators, oppofed to the Roman church.

As to the conftitution and government of the
ftate, after an infinity of propofitions and difcuf-
fions, fuggefted by the variety of interefts, Mont-
lue or Marillac, by the fecret order of the Queen,
propofed an Affembly of the States General : and
the two parties, with one voice confented.   The
Conftable, the Admiral and their partizans, by
the hope of obtaining a change in the miniftry,
the Queen-mother and the Guifes, becaufe they
hoped to deftroy their rivals.   An edict was accordingly paffed at Fontainbleau, for holding the
States General, and the fecretaries of ftate ex-
pedited letters patents to all the Provinces of the
Kingdom, with orders to fend, in the month of
October, their deputies to Orleans, there to hold
the States General.

La Sague took the road to Bearn, charged
with letters and commiffions for the King of
Navarre,

Navarre, from the Conftable, the Admiral and their adherents. At Etampes, he was arrefted and all his papers feized, and brought to court, by order of the Queen and the Guifes. La Sague, interrogated on the rack, confeffed, that the defign of the Prince of Condé, to which the King of Navarre was privy and confenting, was to march from Bearn, under pretext of repairing to court, and to make himfelf mafter in his courfe, of the principal cities of the kingdom, to take poffeffion of Paris by means of the Conftable, and Marfhal Montmorencie his fon, who had the government of it ; to caufe, in the next place to revolt, Picardy, by the intrigues of Senarpont and Bouchavannes ; Brittanny, by thofe of the duke D'Eftampes, who, as governor had a powerful party there. He declared that the Prince was in courfe to come to court, at the head of all the forces of the Hugonots ; oblige the States General to difmifs from the Miniftry, the Queen-mother and the Guifes, to declare that the King cannot be of age, till twenty-two years old, and finally to give him for tutors and regents of the kingdom, the Conftable, the Prince de Condé and the King of Navarre. La Sague added, that by moiftening with water, the covering of the letters of the Vidâme de Chartres, they would fee, in writing, all that he had revealed. The Plan of the enemies of the Princes of Lorrain, was indeed found upon trial, written, upon the cover of the letters of the Vidâme de Chartres, in the proper hand of Flemin D'Ardoy, fecretary of the Conftable. This revelation of the fecret by La Sague, put the court upon a thoufand manœuvres, to ftrengthen their party in the Provinces, but ftill they continued to diffemble their defigns

T   of of vengeance: The Proteſtants ſomewhat encouraged on one hand by hopes, and ſtill tormented with perſecutions on the other, broke out in arms in ſeveral places : But the Prince de Condé, whoſe anxiety muſt have been very great for his preſent ſafety, if his ambition was not as inſatiable, and his natural inquietude as troubleſome as is repreſented, made an attempt to ſeize upon Lyons as a ſtrong hold, and an aſylum for himſelf and a place of arms for his party ; but he miſcarried, and many of his partizans, the poor Hugonots, were executed.

As ſoon as the King was informed of this enterprize, he reſolved not to give the diſcontented leiſure to form new ones. He left Fontainbleau, accompanied with a thouſand lances, and two regiments of old infantry, lately returned from Piedmont and Scotland. He took the road to Orleans, preſſing the deputies of the Provinces, to repair to that city.

The French nation is divided into three orders, or ſtates, the Clergy, the Nobility, and the People. Theſe three orders are diſtributed into thirty diſtricts or juriſdictions, called Bailliages or Senechalſies. When an aſſembly of the States General is to be held, they reſort to the capital of their reſpective Provinces, where they elect each one ſeparately a deputy, who aſſiſts, in the name of his order, at the general aſſembly, and who enters into all the deliberations relative to the particular intereſts of each one of the three orders, and to the general good of the ſtate. Each Bailliage furniſhes three deputies, the firſt for the Clergy, the ſecond for the Nobility, and the third for the People, under the name, which in France was then conſidered as more honourable,

ble, of the third eftate. All thefe deputies affembled in prefence of the King, of the Princes of
the blood, and of the officers of the crown, form
the Body of the States General, and act in the
name of the nation, whofe power and authority
they reprefent.

———————————

No. 21.

——————

————My foul aches,
To know, when two authorities are up,
Neither fupreme, how foon confufion
May enter 'twixt the gap of both, and take
The one by the other.   SHAKESPEAR.

WHEN the King is of age, and affifts at the
States General, the deputies had the power to
confent to his demands ; to propofe what they
judge neceffary for the good of the different orders of the ftate ; to make their fubmiffions in
the name of the people to new impofts ; to eftablifh and accept of new laws, and new regulations ;
but when the minority of the Prince, or fome
other incapacity hinders him to govern by himfelf, the ftates have a right in cafe of conteftation,
to elect the regent of the kingdom, to nominate
to the principal offices, to form a council, and,
if the mafculine pofterity have failed in the royal
family, they may elect a new Monarch, following however, the difpofitions of the falique law.
Excepting thefe cafes of neceffity, the Kings were
accuftomed to affemble the States General, in urgent

gent conjunctures, and to determine, according to their advice, in affairs of moſt importance. " In effect," ſays Davila, " what energy may not the reſolutions of the Prince derive, from the concurrence of his ſubjects ? What can be more conformable to the true ſpirit of monarchical government, than this harmony between the ſovereign and the people ?" In truth, Davila, though thou art a profound Hiſtorian, thou art but a ſuperficial Legiſlator ! Hiſtory anſwers the queſtion, that no energy at all, nor any thing but diviſion, diſtraction and extravagance were derived to the reſolutions of the Prince, till the ſtates were laid aſide. In the language of my motto, two authorities were up, neither ſupreme, and confuſion entered 'twixt the gap. Nothing can be more directly repugnant to monorchical government than ſuch aſſemblies, becauſe they ſet up rivals to the King, and excite doubts and queſtions, in whom the ſovereignty reſides. If a negative is given by them, to the will of the Prince, they become a part of the ſovereignty, annihilate the Monarchy, and convert it into a Republic. If they are mere councils of advice, they become ſcenes of cabal, for aſpiring grandees to force themſelves into the miniſtry.—Never indeed was it more neceſſary to new model the government and regenerate the nation, than in the preſent conjuncture, when the rivalries of the grandees, employing as inſtruments, the differences in religion, diſturbed the whole kingdom, and demanded the prompteſt remedies.

Upon the reiterated orders of the court, the deputies of the Provinces, had reſorted to Orleans, from the beginning of October 1560, and the King having arrived in perſon, accompanied

by

by moſt of the Lords and great officers of the
crown, they waited only for the diſcontented
Lords and Princes, to open the Aſſembly.   The
Conſtable and his ſons, were, as uſual, at Chantilly.   The King of Navarre and the Prince of
Condé, were ſtill at Bearn.   The King had written to them all, to invite them to the States; and
altho they had not explicitly refuſed, they invented pretexts upon pretexts, to excuſe themſelves,
and gain time.   Theſe affected delays diſtreſſed
the King and the miniſtry.   They apprehended,
with reaſon, that the refuſal of the Princes of the
blood, ariſing from their own ſuſpicions, or
upon ſome certain information of what was intended againſt them, would defeat all the projects
and preparations, founded only on the hope that
they would aſſiſt at the States General.   The
Prince of Condé, could not be in doubt that they
had drawn, either from the priſoners of Amboiſe,
or from La Sague, or from the conſpirators ar-
reſted at Lyons, evidence ſufficient to diſcover
his deſigns.   No motive, therefore, could determine him to place himſelf a ſecond time, at the
diſcretion of a court where his enemies were all
powerful.   The King of Navarre thought differ-
ently.   Leſs culpable, or more credulous than his
brother, he believed, that by going to the States,
they ſhould obtain, without difficulty, that reform in the government, which had already coſt
them ſo much labor ; whereas, by refuſing to
be preſent, they would betray their own intereſts,
and leave the field open to the ambition and violence of the Princes of Lorrain.   He could not
believe, that under the eyes of the whole nation
aſſembled, a King ſcarcely out of his infancy, an
Italian Princeſs, and two ſtrangers, would dare
                                              to

to imbrue their hands in the blood of the Princes
of the royal houfe, which the Monarchs the moft
abfolute and the moft vindictive, had ever regarded as facred. All thefe motives determined him
to venture to the States, with the Prince, to
whom he reprefented, that they would infallibly
condemn him unheard, if he continued obftinate-
ly to abfent himfelf from court ; whereas, by
appearing there, and gaining to his interefts the
deputies in the States, there was every reafon to
hope, that if, on judging him with rigor, they
fhould blame his proceedings, the equity of his
pretenfions, would afford him a favourable colour, and in the laft extremity, his birth would
obtain him a pardon. All the confidants and partizans of the Princes, fupported this advice, except the wife and mother-in-law of the Prince of
Condé, who conftantly rejected it, and judged
that his life was aimed at. and that of all the
courfes he could take that which was recommended to him was the moft dangerous.

In the midft of thefe irrefolutions, the King
fent them De Cruffol and Saint Andre, to engage
them to repair to Orleans. Thefe Lords remonftrated to them. that an Affembly fo refpectable,
and which occafioned fo great an expence to the
King and the nation, had not been called but on
their account, and to fatisfy their complaints and
demands : That they were there to deliberate on
the means of reforming the government, and
appeafing the difputes of religion ; matters of fo
high importance, that they could not be decided,
without the prefence and concurrence of the Princes of the blood. That if the Princes of Bourbon,
after having fo often demanded the reformation
of the government, and an examination of the
caufe

cause of the Hugonots, refused to assist at the
States assembled for those purposes, it would seem
that they meant to trifle with the King, and in-
sult the majesty of an assembly which represented the body of the nation. That they ought
hereafter, to impute to themselves alone, their
exclusion from dignities and governments, since
they had not deigned to come and receive the
authority which the King appeared disposed to
grant them, with the concurrence of the States.
That this conduct proving their little attachment
to the service of the King, and the good of the
kingdom, they ought not to be surprized if the
firmest resolutions should be taken to extirpate
the seeds of discord, and manifest designs to dis-
turb the state. That if the King was disposed to
reward such as gave him proofs of their obedience
and fidelity, he was equally determined to reduce
to a forced but necessary submission, those who
should attempt to resist his will, and excite revolts in the cities and Provinces of his kingdom ;
a crime of which he would suspect the Princes of
Bourbon, as long as they should neglect to justify
themselves, and their absence and obstinacy should
confirm, the injurious reports which were spread
concerning them. That hitherto neither the
King nor his Council, had given credit to them ;
but that the King desired that, for the honor of
the royal blood, the Princes would give proofs of
their fidelity and of their zeal for the good of
the state, and would justify the sincerity of their
intentions in the eyes of France, whose attention
was attracted and fixed by the assembly of the
States. These representations made little impression on the Prince of Condé, who was resolved not to risque his person, in a place where
enemies

enemies could do all things. But his firmnefs was, in the end, conftrained to bend
under the neceffity. Cruffol returned to court,
with an account of the averfion of the Prince,
to come to the States. The Guifes advifed to
employ force to determine him. The Queen did
not oppofe it : and the King took the refolution
to conftrain them by force of arms. To this
end they fend de Thermes into Gafcony, and began to form under his command, an army compofed of Gendarmery and all the Infantry diftributed in the neighbouring Provinces.

The Bourbons were without troops, deftitute
of every thing, fhut up in Bearn, a little Province
at the foot of the Pyrennees, wedged in between
France and Spain. They doubted not, that if,
on the one hand the troops of the King affembled
in Gafcony, and on the other, thofe of the King
of Spain, who ardently wifhed to invade the
feeble remains of Navarre, fhould attack them,
they fhould eafily be fubjugated and ftripped of
their dominions. The infurrections which the
Prince of Condé had excited in France, had been
attended with no fuccefs. He was in Bearn
without troops and without money. The King
of Navarre who would not expofe the reft of his
ftates, nor his wife and children, whom he had
about him, yielded to neceffity, more powerful
than any counfels, and finally determined his
brother on the journey to Orleans, in the general perfuafion, that, efpecially during the feffion
of the States, the miniftry would not take any
violent refolution againft them ; whereas, by ob-
ftinately remaining at Bearn, they would expofe
themfelves to the infamy which always accompanies the name of rebels, and ruin themfelves
                                        without

without refource. The Cardinal of Bourbon, their brother, contributed not a little to haften this refolution. The foftnefs and ductility of his character, his averfion to troubles, his tendernefs for his brothers, and the infinuations of the Queen, engaged him to ride poft to Bearn, as foon as he learnt the intentions and preparations of the court, to force the King of Navarre and the Prince of Condé to appear at the States. He ex-aggerated, on one hand, the number of troops deftined againft them, and capable of crufhing them ; and on the other, he affured them, that the King and the Queen, had difcovered none, but favorable difpofitions, and an earneft zeal to re-eftablifh concord and public tranquility. They left, therefore, the Queen Jane and her children, at Pau, and with few attendants, all three together, took the road to Orleans.

The Conftable, whom the court affected to urge lefs, becaufe he was in a place where he might be more eafily compelled, had commenced his journey with more confidence in appearance, but in reality with more precaution. He had not abetted the difcontented but with his coun-fels, which only tended to demand juftice of the States, without plotting confpiracies, or exciting infurrections. A refufal to go to court might fortify the fufpicions conceived againft him : He therefore employed artifice and diffimulation, to delay his arrival and regulate his proceedings by the example of the Princes. Arrived at Paris, he pretended to be attacked with the gout, and re-turned to Chantilly to re-eftablifh his health. He again attempted to proceed, but under the pre-text that the change of air and the motion of the carriage incommoded him, which his advanced

U   age

age rendered plaufible enough ; he travelled by
little day's journeys, frequently by crofs-ways,
at a diftance from the great road, where he made
long delays, to prolong the time, till the arrival
of the Princes. His fons, in perfuading him to
haften his march, reprefented to him, that neither
the Queen mother nor the Guifes would ever
dare to attempt any thing againft a man, fo refpected as he was in the kingdom. The Conftable, inftructed by experience, anfwered them,
that the miniftry could govern the ftate at its
pleafure, and without oppofition, though they
feemed to be preparing for themfelves a formidable one, by calling the States General. That this
conduct inveloped fome myfterious intrigue,
which he fhould be able to unveil, with a little
patience. This judicious reflection abated the
ardor of the young Lords, and the Conftable continued to temporize.

Neverthelefs the King of Navarre and the
Prince of Condé had been received on the frontiers by the Marfhal de Thermes, who, under the
pretext of paying them the honors due to their
rank, followed them with a large body of Cavalry, to make fure of the cities become fufpected
by the depofition of La Sague. At the fame
time, he ordered poffeffion to be taken by other
troops, both of Cavalry and Infantry, of all the
roads, which the Princes left behind them, left a
change of their refolution fhould determine them
to return. As foon as it was known at court,
that the Princes had entered the kingdom, and
were fo well obferved by De Thermes, they arrefted, all on a fudden, Jerome Grollot, Bailif of
Orleans, accufed of intelligence with the Hugonots, to caufe a revolt of that city in favor of the
difcontented

difcontented Princes ; and by order of the King, they fent to prifon the Vidâme of Chartres, who had been imprudent enough to remain in the Capital. They had not the fame fuccefs in attempting to feize Dandelot. As prudent and fubtle in providing againft dangers, as ardent and daring in forming defigns, he retired fuddenly to the coafts of Brittany, refolved to embark for England in cafe of neceffity. The Admiral Coligni, whofe addrefs and diffimulation, according to Davila, had hitherto conducted every thing, without difcovering or expofing himfelf, was among the firft in the States General, with defign there to labor in favor of his party. The King and the Queen had received him as ufual, with benevolence. He employed himfelf in following with his eye, all the meafures of the court, in order to give information of them, fecretly, and with extreme precautions, to the Conftable and the King of Navarre.

All thefe delays were exhaufted, when the Princes of the blood arrived at Orleans, the 29th of October, without any perfon's going out to receive them, except a fmall number of their moft intimate friends. They found not only the gates of the city guarded, but bodies of guards placed and batteries erected in the ftrongeft pofts, in the crofs ftreets and public places ; precautions which the court had not ufually taken in times of war. They paffed through the midft of this formidable apparatus, and came to the King's Lodge, where they kept a more exact guard, than at the head-quarters of an army. Arrived at the gate, they would have entered on horfeback, according to the right attached to their

rank ;

rank: but they found only a wicket gate open, and were obliged to alight in the open ſtreet, and few perſons appeared to receive or ſalute them. They were conducted to the King, whom they found ſitting between the Duke of Guiſe and the Cardinal of Lorrain, ſurrounded by the Captains of his guards. He received the King of Navarre and the Prince of Condé, with a coldneſs very different from that affability which the Kings of France are accuſtomed to practice to all their ſubjects, but above all to the Princes of their blood. He conducted them ſoon to the Queen-mother, where the Guiſes did not follow them. Catharine of Medicis, who wiſhed always to appear neuter and diſintereſted, received them with ordinary demonſtrations of friendſhip, but with an affected ſorrow, and artificial tears. The King continued to treat them with the ſame coldneſs, and addreſſing himſelf to the Prince of Condé, he began to reproach him, that without having received from his Majeſty, either diſpleaſure or ill treatment, he had in contempt of all laws, divine and human, excited ſeveral times his ſubjects, inkindled a war in different parts of his kingdom, attempted to ſeize on his principal cities, and conſpired againſt his life, and that of his brothers. The Prince, without emotion, anſwered with firmneſs, that theſe accuſations were ſo many calumnies forged by his enemies. We muſt proceed then, replied the King, by the ordinary ways of juſtice, to diſcover the truth. He went out of the apartment of the Queen, and commanded the Captains of his guards to arreſt the Prince of Condé. The Queen-mother, forced to conſent to this meaſure, but who had not forgotten that things might change, from one moment

ment to another, exerted herself to console the King of Navarre. The Prince complained of none but the Cardinal of Bourbon his brother, who had deceived him ; and suffered himself to be conducted to a neighbouring house, destined for his prison. They had walled up the windows, doubled the doors, and made it a kind of fortress defended by several pieces of artillery and a strong guard. The King of Navarre, astonished at the detention of his brother, breathed out his grief in complaints and reproaches to the Queen, who, casting all the blame on the Duke of Guise, as Lieutenant General of the Kingdom, endeavored only to exculpate herself. To the King of Navarre, they gave for a lodging, an house, at a little distance from that which the King occupied, and guards to observe his motions ; so that, excepting the liberty of seeing whom he pleased, he was in all other respects treated and confined like a prisoner. At the same time they arrested Bouchar this secretary, with all his letters and papers ; and Madeleine de Roye, mother-in-law of the Prince, with all her letters and papers, at her seat at Anisi. Although they held the gates of Orleans shut, and suffered no person to go out, the news of these transactions were announced to the Constable, who was still but a few leagues from Paris. He suspended his journey, resolved to pass no further, but to wait and observe the consequences of these events.

Thus the mystery suspected by the Constable was unriddled. The States General were summoned only as a net is laid, artfully to be sprung upon game. This game were the Constable and Princes, and their principal friends. They were a mere stalking-horse, behind which to shoot a wood-cock ;

wood-cock ; and that wood-cock was the Prince of Condé. Although of the two authorities which were up, the Court and the States, neither was fupreme ; yet the one we fee might be taken by the other. We fhall foon fee that confufion entered by the gap.

No. 22.

Interveonit deinde, his cogitationibus, avitum malum, regni cupido, atque inde fædum certamen coortum.

THE Queen-mother and the Guifes, delayed no longer the opening of the States. They began by the profeffion of faith, drawn up by the Sorbonne, conformably to the doctrine of the Roman Catholic Church. The Cardinal de Tournon, Prefident of the order of the Clergy, read it with a loud voice, and each of the deputies approved and adhered to it, upon oath : a precaution which they judged neceffary to affure themfelves of the catholicity of thofe who were to have a deliberative voice, in the general affembly. After this folemn act, the Chancellor propofed, in the prefence of the King, the matters which were to be taken into confideration. *At the inftance of the Provinces, the three orders feparated, to examine the refpective demands, and make report of their refolutions.* But all this was merely theatrical : it was nothing but farcical fcenery. The Guifes knew, as well as the Conftable de Montmorency, that the

the miniftry could govern the kingdom, and nation at its will, as a Court or hereditary Supreme Executive always will, where it is checked only by a fingle reprefentative affembly, efpecially if that affembly have no authority but to advife, unlefs it has recourfe to violence. Nay, if it have Legiflative authority, the majority in that affembly can only govern, by impofing its own men on the Executive, in other words, by forcing the King to take their creatures into the miniftry. So that the miniftry and the majority in the National Affembly muft always act in concert, and be agreed; and they generally are fo, to the intolerable oppreffion of the minority, as in this cafe, until the minority rife in arms. Reformation of government, and liberty of confcience, and redrefs of grievances in religion, were fubjects which the court had too much cunning to bring before the Affembly. That would have been, as the Conftable expreffed it, to have prepared a formidable oppofition to themfelves. Had the point been then fettled, that the States were a Legiflative Affembly; and had the queftion of religion been brought fairly into deliberation and difcuffion before them, it is very probable that liberty of confcience to the Hugonots, might have been the refult, even in that age. But thefe, as Davila fays, were the fmalleft objects they had in view: all minds expected with much more folicitude, the iffue of the detenfion of the Prince of Condé. Their doubts were foon refolved by a declaration of council figned by the King, the Chancellor and all the grandees, except the Guifes, who, as fufpected of partiality, affected not to appear in this affair. A commiffion was eftablifhed for the trial of the Prince, with authority to render a definitive

definitive fentence. De Thou, prefident, and Faye and Viole, counfellors of the Parliament of Paris, were the Judges—Bourdin, Attorney General, Tillot, Secretary: All the interrogations and acts were done in the prefence of the Chancellor L'Hopital. They heard the depofitions of the prifoners of Amboife, Lyons and others. They made preparations to interrogate the Prince. He refufed to anfwer, alledging that in quality of Prince of the blood, he acknowledged no other tribunal, than the Parliament of Paris. He demanded an affembly of all the chambers of Parliament ; that the King fhould be prefent in perfon, and that the twelve Peers fhould have a voice, as well as the great officers of the crown, according to the ancient ufage. That he could not excufe himfelf, for not remonftrating againft a proceeding fo unheard of, and irregular, and from appealing to the King. This appeal was carried to council, and appeared authorized by reafon, by the ordinary formalities, and by the cuftoms of the kingdom. But the fpirit of rivalry, which is the fpirit of party, demanded a fudden vengeance : a party at prefent triumphant, but doubtful whether it were at bottom the moft powerful, were impelled by fear, as well as hatred, to wifh a prompt decifion. The appeal was declared null. But the Prince, having renewed it, and perfifted in his proteftations, the council, at the motion of the Attorney-General, pronounced that they ought to confider the Prince as convicted, fince he refufed to anfwer to commiffioners named by the King. In this manner they obliged him to fubmit to interrogatories, and purfued the trial, without lofs of time, to final judgment.

The Princes of Bourbon, at the fummit of misfortune,

misfortune, were very near expiating with their blood, the heinous crime of daring to ftand in competition with the Guifes, to patronize liberty of confcience, and to fhelter from perfecution the diftreffed Hugonots : as Manlius was precipitated from the Tarpeian Rock, for being the friend of the oppreffed debtors, and the rival of Camillus and the Quintian family. Both were accufed, it is true, with crimes againft the ftate. The fplendor of the birth of the two Bourbons, and their perfonal merit, interefted all France. Even their enemies pitied their deftiny. The Guifes alone, naturally enterprizing, purfued conftantly their defigns, without regard to the merit or quality of thofe Princes, whether they judged fuch an act of feverity abfolutely neceffary, to the fafety and tranquility of the kingdom, or whether, as their enemies fuppofed, they had nothing in view but the deftruction of their rivals, and the eftablifhment of their own grandeur. They declared openly, that it was neceffary by two ftrokes, at the fame time, to ftrike off the heads of Herefy and Rebellion. *Such is the fpirit of fophiftry : and fuch is the fpirit of party.* The Queen-mother, although fhe confented fecretly, and wifhed that the refolution taken at Amboife, of deftroying the Princes, fhould be executed, defired neverthelefs, that all the odium of it fhould fall upon the Guifes, as fhe had always had the addrefs, to accomplifh. She propofed to manage the two parties, for fear of thofe unforefeen events, which the inconftancy of fortune might produce ; and affected much grief and melancholly in her behaviour, and referve in her difcourfe. She had even frequent conferences with the two Chatillons, the Admiral and Cardinal,

w in

in which fhe appeared difpofed to feek fome expedient, to extricate from danger the Princes of
the blood. She amufed in the fame manner, the
Dutchefs of Montpenfier, a Princefs full of the
beft intentions, an enemy of all diffimulation,
and who judged of the characters of others by
the rectitude of her own. Her inclination to
Calvinifm, and her intimate connections with
the King of Navarre, had enabled her to com-
mence and continue between that Prince and
the Queen, a fecret correfpondence. Thefe intrigues, although directly oppofite to the conduct
which the court held in public, were palliated
with fo much artifice, that the moft clear-fighted,
could not unravel their genuine defign, even
when they reflected on the depths of the fecrets
of mankind, and the diverfity of interefts and
paffions which ferve as motives to their actions.

Already the commiffioners had rendered their
judgment againft the Prince of Condé. They
had condemned him, as convicted of high treafon
and rebellion, to be beheaded, before the palace
of the King, at the hour of the affembly of the
States General. They delayed the execution,
only to draw into the fame fnare the Conftable,
who, in fpight of the repeated inftances of the
court, ftill delayed his journey to the States.
They wifhed to involve in the fame profcription
the King of Navarre, but they had not proofs
againft him, fufficient to fatisfy their own creatures, when one morning the King, in dreffing
himfelf, fell all at once into a fwoon, fo deep, and
violent, that his officers believed him to be dead.
He recovered his fenfes, it is true : but his malady
was judged to be mortal, and his life was defpaired of.   This fatal mifchance terrified the Guifes.
                                        They

They preffed the Queen-mother, to execute the
fentence againft the Prince of Condé, while the
breath remained in the body of the King, and to
take the fame refolution againft the King of
Navarre, to prevent all the revolutions which
they might have to fear, in cafe of the King's
death. They reprefented to her, with warmth,
that this was the fole means of preferving the
crown to her other infant children, and of diffi-
pating the ftorm which menaced France: that,
although the Conftable was not arrefted, and in
the prefent delicate circumftances, it would not
be prudent to feize him, yet that when they
fhould have no longer to fear, neither the credit,
nor the pretenfions of the Princes of the blood,
the Conftable would be lefs formidable, as he
would neither have the nobility in his interefts
nor the Hugonots of his party : that to deliberate
in the moment of execution, and fufpend it in
this critical fituation of the King, would be to
lofe the fruit of fo many projects conducted to
their end, with fo much artifice and patience :
that even the death of the King ought not to be
an obftacle, becaufe that brothers fucceeding him
of right, the fame reafons and the fame interefts
ftill fubfifted, both for them and their mother.
The Queen who had known how to preferve
herfelf neuter, at leaft in appearance, and who
had not motives fo urgent to precipitate meafures, confidered that under a minority, Kings
might change their afpect, and that the exceffive
grandeur of the Guifes remaining without oppofition, might become to her as formidable as the
ambition of the Princes of the blood. Thus,
fometimes by fuppofing the diftemper of the
King to be lefs dangerous, fometimes by fpreading

ing favorable reports of a fpeedy cure, fhe gained time, delayed the execution of the Prince, and referved the liberty of acting according to circumftances, conformably to thofe views, in which fhe was confirmed by the councils of the Chancellor de L'Hofpital. As foon as fhe had known that the King's life was in danger, fhe requefted the fon of the Duke de Montpenfier, to conduct her fecretly one night into the apartment of the King of Navarre, and in a long converfation which fhe had with him, fhe endeavored, with her ordinary diffimulation, to perfuade him, that fhe was very far from approving all that had paffed, and wifhed to act in concert with him, to oppofe the ambition of the Guifes. The Prince depended little on the fincerity of thefe proteftations : they had however an effect in the fequel. On the fifth of December the King died.

Charles the ninth, fecond fon of the Queen, fucceeded to Francis the fecond, his brother. He was but eleven years of age, and muft have a tutor, and the Kingdom a regent.

No. 23.

Utrumque regem, fua multitudo confalutaverat.

EACH party expected its own regent. The ancient ufage, and laws often confirmed by the States, called of right to the function, the King of Navarre. But what a reverfe ? What an appearance ? To confide the perfon of the young
King,

King, and the government of the kingdom to a
Prince fufpected of a confpiracy againft the ftate,
detained as a prifoner, and the accomplice of a
brother condemned to death !

The *Guifes* had governed with fupreme authority under the late King, and attempted the moft
violent meafures.   By committing to them the
fame power, it was eafy to follow the fame plan
and execute the fame defigns.   But they were
not of the royal blood : how, commit to them
the tutorage of a young King, contrary to all the
laws of the monarchy ? What envy, what jealoufy, what oppofitions would they not have to
contend with, from the nobility and the grandees,
who would be difcontented with their power,
and afpire to defpoil them of it ?

The States had fometimes confided the regency to the mothers of Kings, during their minority, and in the prefent competition of fo many
interefts and contending factions, it was not prudent to place in other hands, the life of the
King, and the confervation of the ftate.—But a
woman, a ftranger, without partifans, and without fupport, could fhe maintain her ground a-
gainft two fuch powerful factions, ready to fupport their pretenfions by the force of arms ?
The *Guifes*, forefeeing what might eafily happen,
leagued themfelves with the Cardinal de *Tournon*,
the Duke de *Nemours*, the Marfhals de *Briffac* and
Saint Andre, *Sippiere*, governor of Orleans, and
many other great Lords, with whofe influence
they reinforced their party, to defend their lives
and preferve their power.   The King of Navarre,
conceiving happier hopes for the future, united,
more ftrictly than ever, with the *Chatillons*, the
Admiral and Cardinal, the Prince de *Porcien*,
Jarnac,

Jarnac, and many others of their partifans. He fecretly armed his friends, and difpatched couri- er after courier to the Conftable. The two par- ties, having thus placed themfelves in a pofture of defence, the whole court, and the troops di- vided themfelves among them, and even the de- puties of the States took their party, each one followed his paffions, his intereft, or his princi- ples.

Never did the neceffity of a third mediating power, or an umpire, appear more plainly than in this cafe. Had there been a conftitution in France, and had that conftitution provided, as it ought to have done, a third party, whofe intereft and duty it fhould have been to do juftice to the other two, and every individual of each, there would have been little danger to the peace, li- berty or happinefs of the people : for fuch an in- termediate authority, by doing juftice to all fides, would have been joined and fupported by the honeft and virtuous of all fides, and by this means would have controuled both parties by the laws. But in this inftance it feemed impoffible to form a third party. Agitation and terror reigned every where. It was dreaded every moment that the friends of the King of Navarre, and thofe of the *Guifes* would come to blows. All their meafures and devices tended mutually to deftroy each other. Nature itfelf, however, without much aid from any conftitution, pro- duced an effect. Although this unbridled ardor of ruling, inflamed as it was by private animofi- ties, hindered not the two parties from render- ing publickly their obedience to the King, this fubmiffion had no other principle than a jealoufy and mutual apprehenfion, that the one party would

would fnatch from the other the firft place in the government. This motive only, and not any refpect for a conftitution, had made both parties eager to appear to be the firft to do homage to Charles the IXth, and on the day of the death of his brother, he was unanimoufly recognized as lawful fovereign. This ftep tended infenfibly to re-eftablifh order and authority. The Queen-mother faw that it would not be fafe to truft the life of her young children, nor the adminiftration of the ftate, to either of the parties, one of which was extremely irritated and embittered, and the other full of affurance and haughty pretenfions, both well fupported and ready to proceed to the laft extremities. She defired to continue miftrefs of her children, and of the government of the ftate : She propofed, to this end, to remain as a mediatrix ; and thought that the two parties, unable to agree among themfelves, and neither being able to triumph over the other, they would both unite in her favor, and abandon to her, by concert, an authority which the oppofition of their competitors would hinder them from obtaining for themfelves. We fee in this inftance that the tripple balance, is fo eftablifhed by providence in the conftitution of nature, that order, without it, can never be brought out of anarchy and confufion. The laws therefore fhould eftablifh this equilibrium, as the dictate of nature and the ordinance of providence.

Catharine hoped, that by conducting with ability, the reins of the ftate would return to her hands. She firft thought of making fure of the Princes of Lorrain. A negotiation fo delicate and thorny, ought not to be confided to any but the

the ableſt hands. The Queen, after having caſt her eyes on ſeveral perſons, fixed them at laſt on the Marſhal *de Saint Andre*, as the man of the court the moſt proper to aſſure her ſucceſs. She ſent for him, and after ſeveral diſcourſes, the reſult was, that it would be impoſſible to terminate the differences of the two parties, without tumult and war, but by relaxing ſomewhat of their pretenſions, by ceding a part on both ſides, and making the Queen the arbitratrix of their intereſt. That by this plan, the two parties, without yielding one to the other, would appear, from reſpect, and for the peace of the public, to give way to the mother of their King, who ſhould hold the equilibrium between the *Guiſes* and the *Bourbons*.

The Queen was a politician refined enough to pretend that ſhe was indebted for this council to the prudence of the Marſhal, rather than that ſhe had ſuggeſted it to him, which was the fact. The Marſhal, judging without paſſion, that this project would be very convenient to the ſlippery and perilous ſituation in which the *Guiſes* ſtood, undertook to negotiate with their party. Upon the propoſition which he made of it to the Duke and Cardinal, and which they brought into deliberation in an aſſembly of their confidents; the opinion of theſe, and even of the two brothers, were divided. The Duke, who had more caution and moderation than his brother, yielded to the accommodation, which was to leave him in poſſeſſion of the governments and riches which he held from the liberality of the late Kings. But the Cardinal more ambitious and more violent, rejected all compromiſes, and pretended that they would preſerve their power in the

fame

fame degree, as they had exercifed it under Francis IId. The fentiment of the Duke was approved by the Cardinal *de Tournon*, the Marfhals *Briffac* and *Saint Andre*, and above all, by *Sepiere*, the
advice of all which perfonages had a weight,
which accompanies an high reputation for prudence juftly acquired. All judged it fufficient
for the *Guifes* to preferve their credit and honors,
and preferve themfelves for circumftances more
favorable ; and the refult they communicated to
the Queen by *Saint Andre*, and left to her the
choice of means the moft proper to treat wijh
the King of Navarre.

There remained ftill a greater obftacle to overcome : to appeafe the faction of the difcontented
Princes ; an enterprize which many thought
impoffible and chimerical : but the Queen, who
perfectly knew the characters and difpofitions of
the perfons with whom fhe had to treat, did not
defpair of obtaining her end. The King of Navarre had for his principal confidents, *Defcars*,
Gafcon, and *Leoncourt*, Bifhop of Auxerre. *Defcars* had a contracted genius and little experience ;
Leoncourt was a defigning politician, but folely in-
tent upon his own fortune. The Queen fecretly
gained both, by approaching each on his weak
fide. She dazzled *Defcars* with prefents, and a-
mufed him with fpecious reafonings. And fhe
excited in the Bifhop of Auxerre, hopes of ecclefiaftical benefices and dignities which he could
not eafily obtain by the fole credit of the King of
Navarre. They both promifed, under the pretext of giving faithful and fincere council to their
mafter, to favor the negotiations which tended
to bring the two parties together, and commit
the regency to the Queen-Mother.

x   The

The Dutchefs of *Montpenfier*, carried the firft propofals of accommodation. Her candor and franknefs, had gained the confidence of the Queen of Navarre. In the progrefs of things, *Carrouges* and *Lanfac*, Lords of confummate prudence, entered infenfibly into this negotiation. By means of thefe perfons the Queen propofed to the King of Navarre three conditions. 1. To fet at liberty all who had been arrefted for the confpiracy of Amboife, the Prince of *Conde*, Madam *de Roye*, and the Vidâme *de Chartres ;* and to annul by the Parliament of Paris, the fentence againft the Prince. 2. To create the King of Navarre, lieutenant-general of the kingdom, on condition that the Queen had the title and authority of regent. 3. To obtain of the King of Spain the reftitution of Navarre. The confidents of the King of Navarre, exaggerated to him thefe advantages ; they reprefented to him that the name of regent, a title without reality, was but an empty and fpecious found, for which he would be abundantly recompenfed by the power and authority, which would be given him over the provinces ; prerogatives in which confifted the effective government of the kingdom. That the glory of delivering the Prince of *Conde*, by the humiliation of his enemies, joined to the hope of re-eftablifhing forever his houfe, in its original fplendor, left him no room to hefitate. It is not a time, faid they, to conteft with rigor againft enemies fo powerful. You have to combat the prejudices, which your enterprizes againft the ftate have excited. Why, upon the brink of a precipice, do you indulge chimerical hopes ? *The deputies of the ftates are almoft all, devoted to the will of the Queen and the* Guifes, *who have chofen them*

them at their pleasure and gained them to their inter-ests. If the affair is left to their decision, it is to be feared that their partiality, will incline them to exclude the Princes from the government, and commit it to the *Guises*, which would infallibly accomplish the final ruin of the house of *Bourbon.*

These reasons shook the resolution of the King of Navarre, and disposed him to follow these councils : but he was still restrained by the Prince of *Conde*, whose keen resentment and desire of vengeance, rather than solid reasons, excited to advise the contrary. The Duke *de Montpensier* and the Prince *de la Rhoche-sur-yon*, supported those who negotiated an accommodation. Both were of the house of *Bourbon*, but of a branch more distant from the royal-stock, and had not meddled in these troubles.

The King of Navarre, before he concluded with the Queen, demanded of her by the immediate negotiators, two new conditions. 1. That they should take away from the *Guises* all the employments they had at court. 2. That liberty of conscience should be given to the Hugonots. From the time that *Calvin* had begun to preach and to write, the first seeds of his doctrines had been sown in the court of Henry, King of Navarre, and Margaret of Valois, his consort, father and mother of the Queen Jane ; and as the minds of these Princes were indisposed to the See of Rome, which had stripped them of their states, under pretext of an excommunication, fulminated by the Pope, Julius the second, against France, and its allies ; in the number of whom was the King of Navarre ; they were easily persuaded of a doctrine contrary to the authority of the Pope, and

and which taught that the cenfures by which they had loft their ftates, were null. The Calviniftical minifters, frequenting the court of thefe Princes, there taught their opinions, which had caft fo deep roots into the mind of Queen Jane, that fhe had abandoned the Catholic faith to embrace Calvinifm. Since her marriage with Anthony of Bourbon, fhe perfifted in the fame fentiments. She had nearly converted her hufband, by the vehement eloquence of *Theodore Beza*, *Peter Martin Vermilly*, and other minifters who retired into Bearn, there to preach their opinions in full liberty. The Prince of *Conde* the admiral, and the other chiefs of the party of the Princes of the blood, having alfo embraced Calvinifm, fome with fincerity, and others to difguife their political views, under the pretext of religion, the King of Navarre perfifted more conftantly than ever, to declare himfelf protector of the Hugonots. For this reafon, he demanded that they fhould grant to the Calvinifts liberty of confcience, as an effential condition of the treaty, opened with the Queens. This Princefs anfwered that to deprive the *Guifes* of the dignities they held at court, would be to go directly againft the agreement which was in negotiation, and the refolution taken to reftore the tranquility of the Kingdom. That thefe Lords who were very powerful, and actually armed, would not endure an affront fo public and outrageous : but that, fupported by the Catholics and the majority·of the ftates, they would exert all their forces and efforts, to maintain their ground. She promifed however to employ, in due time, all her addrefs, to diminifh their credit and power. As to the liberty of confcience, fhe convinced them that it

was

was a point too delicate, to be granted all at once : That the Parliaments and even the States, would not fail to oppofe it : But fhe promifed, in fecret, that in governing with the King of Navarre, fhe would labor in concert with him, by indirect and concealed ways, to feize all favorable occafions to grant to the reformed all the liberty of confcience that might be poffible. The Queen, yielding to the neceffity of the conjuncture, gave thefe promifes, without any intention to obferve them : She therefore delayed the execution of them, with all her addrefs. In fact, fhe knew, or at leaft believed, that nothing was more contrary to the grandeur and intereft of her children, than totally to deprefs the *Guifes*, who ferved, admirably well, the purpofe of balancing the power of the Princes of the blood. On the other hand, the liberty of confcience granted to the Hugonots, would have offended the See of Rome, and the other Catholic Princes, and fcattered forever, as fhe pretended, diforder and diffention in the kingdom.

The coalition was on the point of conclufion, when the King of Navarre declared that he would determine nothing, without the advice and confent of the Conftable, who had cured all his gouts, fluxions and rheums, or in other words, difmiffed his pretexts, and approached Orleans. It was therefore neceffary to invent new projects, to furmount this obftacle, which many imagined the moft difficult of all. The Queen knew to the bottom, the character of the Conftable, and that nothing flattered him more, than the part of umpire or moderator in every thing that paffed around him. She thought that by reftoring him the fupreme command of the army, and

by

by affuring him, that it was from him that fhe
wifhed to hold her own grandeur, and the fafety
of her children ; fhe would fix him eafily in her
intereft, and detach him equally from both parties.   Thus, with the advice of the King of Navarre, and the *Guifes*, who were returning to
pacific fentiments, and feemed to fubmit all to
her will ; fhe ordered the captains of the guards,
and the governor of Orleans to furrender to the
Conftable, at his entrance into the city, the command of the armies, and to acknowledge him for
their chief.   Thefe marks of honor awakened in
the breaft of Anne of Montmorency, the ancient
fentiments of devotion and fidelity, which had
attached him for fo many years to the father and
grand-father of the King.   Arrived at Orleans,
he turned to the captains and faid, with his ordinary dignity, that fince the King had reftored
him his command, they might difpenfe with
guarding his Majefty fo exactly in full peace ;
and that without employing the force of arms,
he would make his mafter refpected through the
whole kingdom and by all his fubjects.   Arrived
at the palace, where the Queen loaded him with
honors, he rendered his homage to the young
King, and with tears in his eyes, conjured him
to fear nothing from the prefent troubles, for
that he and all good Frenchmen, were ready to
facrifice their lives for the fupport of his crown.
The Queen encouraged by this difcourfe, the firft
proof of the fuccefs of her contrivances, entered
without delay into fecret conferences with the
Conftable, before that others had time to entertain and to gain him.   She protefted that fhe expected every thing from him, both for her children and herfelf ; *that the royal authority and the*
                                                public

public good were no longer but idle names, for two factions embittered against each other, for their mutual destruction ; that she despaired of preserving to her children under age, a crown envied and attacked by such powerful enemies ; unless his fidelity, of which he had so long given such shining proofs, should cause him to embrace the defence of the young monarch, of a kingdom torn with divisions, and of all the royal family. These words in the mouth of a woman, a mother, a Queen in affliction, made so deep an impression on the mind of the Constable, that he consented to the accommodation ready to be concluded with the King of Navarre. Flattered with the humiliation of the *Guises,* and re-established in the functions of the first trust in the kingdom, he renounced all interests of faction, and resolved to unite with the Queen, for the preservation of the state, in which he aspired only to reassume the place which he had merited by his long services.

Concord being thus established, by the authority of the Constable, they assembled the council : All the Princes and officers of the crown assisted at it ; and the Chancellor having, according to custom, made the propositions in presence of the King, they concluded unanimously that the Queen should be declared regent of the kingdom, the King of Navarre lieutenant-general in the Provinces : the Constable, generalissimo of the armies, the Duke of *Guise,* grand-master of the King's houshold, and the Cardinal *de Lorrain,* superintendant of the finances.

The Prince of *Conde* was now discharged from Prison, and an Arret of the Parliament of Paris, conceived in honorable terms, discharged him from all the accusations against him ; and the
fentence

fentence declared null and irregular, as the work of judges incompetent in the caufe of the Princes of the blood. The Vidame *de Chartres*, died of chagrin in the Baftile, before the coalition was finifhed. Thus ended the year 1560.

In the beginning of the year 1561, the Queen-mother and the King of Navarre difmiffed the States General, leaft the *Guifes* fhould excite fome fermentation there. The formation of a conftitution and the fettlement of religion, were never the real objects for which they had been called. It appears not that they were even afked to ratify the regency in the Queen-mother. So loofe and uncertain was the fovereignty of that great nation, that a confufed agreement of the chiefs of the two factions, was thought fufficient for its government, without any forms or legal folemnities. The ftability of the government, and the fecurity of the lives, liberties and properties of the people was proportionate to fuch a fyftem. The court was ftill agitated with divifions and diffentions.

The *Guifes*, who had obtained but a fmall part of their pretenfions ; that is to fay, much in appearance and little in reality ; accuftomed to rule, and very difcontented with the government and with the Queen, who failed to perform the promifes fhe had made to them watched all opportunities to regain their firft advantages. The Prince of *Conde*, more irritated than ever, kept in view his ancient projects, and burned with an implacable defire of vengeance. The *Colignies* were obftinate to protect the Hugonots. The two parties labored to gain the Conftable, but he declared that he would remain neuter, and attach himfelf

himfelf only to the King and the Queen. He was confirmed in this refolution by the conduct of the King of Navarre, who, fatisfied with the prefent arrangement, lived in good intelligence with the regent, and thought of nothing but peace. The Admiral, his brothers, and the Prince of *Conde*, flattered themfelves that the connection of blood would draw the Conftable, ultimately to their party. The *Guifes*, who knew his attachment to the Catholic faith, and his averfion to Calvinifm, which he had cruelly perfecuted under Henry IId, defpaired not to gain him, under the pretext of defending religion, and exterminating the Hugonots. The vivacity of the King of Navarre, in urging the Queen to accomplifh the promifes fhe had made him in favor of the Hugonots, contributed not a little to keep up this fermentation. This Princefs, fatiffied with having eftablifhed a kind of equilibrium, which fecured her power and that of her children, dreaded to intercept it, and avoided all occafions of difpleafing the King of Navarre.

She made ufe of delays and pretexts, in hopes that the King of Navarre would relax ; but that Prince, excited and tranfported beyond the bounds of his character, by the continued inftigations of his brother, and the Admiral, and by the urgent folicitations of the Queen his confort, became the more ardent in demanding what had been promifed him. The Chancellor *De L'Hopital*, whether he judged a liberty of confcience neceffary to the good of the ftate, or whether he had an inclination to Calvinifm, favored, under hand, the folicitations of the King of Navarre. He reftrained with all his authority, the feverity of the other magiftrates, and exhorted the Queen

Y

to be fparing of blood, to leave confciences in tranquility, and to avoid every thing which might interrupt a peace, which had coft fo much pains to eftablifh. Several of thofe who compofed the council, fupported thefe inftances of the King of Navarre, and protefted that they ought to be weary of imbruing their hands in the blood of Frenchmen ; and that it was time to put an end to punifhments, the fear of which forced fo many good fubjects to abandon their houfes, families and country. The Hugonots themfelves, among whom were many perfons of fenfe and merit, neglected no cares nor means proper to favor their caufe ; and fometimes by writing compofed with art, and fkilfully propagated ; fometimes by petitions prefented in proper feafons ; and fometimes by perfuafive difcourfes of their partizans, endeavored ro imprefs the great in their favor, by pathetic paintings of the misfortunes with which they were opprefled. The Queen was, at length, obliged to give way to the fentiments and authority of fo many perfons. Perhaps fhe was convinced of the wifdom of relaxing a feverity, which fhe was in no condition to maintain ; and of abandoning laws, which they could no longer execute with rigour. She confented therefore to an Edict, rendered by the council on the 28th of January. This Edict enjoined all magiftrates to releafe all the prifoners arrefted, on account of religion ; to ftop all profecutions commenced for this caufe ; to hinder difputes upon matters of faith ; forbidding individuals to give each other the odious appellations of Heretics or Papifts : finally, to prevent unlawful affemblies, commotions, feditions, and maintain concord and peace in all their departments.

Thus,

Thus, with the defign of putting an end to punifhments and the effufion of blood, a motive dictated by religion and humanity, Calvinifm was, if not permitted, at leaft tolerated, and indirectly authorifed.

More lively conteftations were expected concerning the promife which refpected the *Guifes*. The King of Navarre, recalling to the Queen the fecret promifes which fhe had made to him, pretended, that in his quality of lieutenant-general of the kingdom, they ought to deliver to him the keys of the palace which the Duke of *Guife* kept, as grand mafter of the King's houfehold.

The Queen, in truth. no longer doubted the attachment of the King of Navarre, and of the Conftable ; but fhe was not ignorant of the increafing coldnefs of the *Guifes*, and delayed with all her artifice the moment of offending them. She wifhed, on one hand, to manage the Hugonots, protected by the Admiral and the Prince of *Conde ;* and on the other, the Catholicks, united under the Duke of *Guife* and the Cardinal of *Lorrain.* Thefe two factions, were like two powerful dikes, under the fhelter of which, fhe enjoyed a calm. By weakening the Catholicks, fhe was afraid of putting the Hugonots in a condition to give her the law. Sometimes by temporizing, therefore, and fometimes by granting other favors to the King of Navarre, fhe eudeavored to divert him from this pretenfion. But the more fhe endeavored to make him lofe fight of this object, the more the Prince purfued it with warmth.

Finally, the Queen, that fhe might not deftroy the harmony fhe had taken fo much pains to eftablifh, commanded the captains of the guards, no longer to carry the keys of the palace to the grand mafter of the King's houfe-hold, but to the lieutenant-general of the kingdom, to whom this prerogative belonged of right. This proceeding irritated the Duke of *Guife*, but infinitely more the Cardinal of *Lorrain*, his brother, lefs becaufe they confidered it as an affront, from which the regulation of the council of regency would have fcreened them, than becaufe they faw clearly, that with the confent of the Queen, the King of Navarre afpired to diftrefs, and deftroy them. They knew very well that they were accufed of liftening to nothing but their intereft and ambition, and feeing themfelves no longer able to prevail in this private quarrel with the Princes of the blood, who difpofed of all the forces, as well as of the royal authority, they diffembled their refentments, and complained of nothing but the liberty of confcience, which had been tacitly granted to the Hugonots, covering thus with the fpecious veil, and the pretext of religion, their paffions and perfonal interefts. Thus the difcords of the great confounded themfelves infenfibly with the differences of religion, and the factions of the Princes, quitting the name of malcontents and Guifards, to affume the more impofing titles of Catholics and Hugonots, they exerted themfelves with the greater fury, as they difguifed it under the names of zeal and of piety.

The regent and the Conftable, mafters of the perfon and authority of the King, held the balance in the middle. The Conftable was indeed much oppofed to Calvinifm, and attached to the Catholic religion ; neverthelefs, his affection for his nephews, and the love of peace, induced him to confent to make ufe of management in matters

of

of religion, until the King fhould arrive at his majority. But to corroborate more and more, the authority of the young monarch, though a minor, thofe who held the reins of government thought proper to conduct him to Reims, where they preferve with veneration, *the Phial which a pigeon brought down from heaven, full of holy oil, with which* Clovis *was anointed and confecrated.*

During the ceremony of confecration, there arofe a new conteft concerning precedency, between the Princes of the blood and the Duke of *Guife.* The former pretended that it was due to their birth. The Duke on his fide demanded it, as firft peer of France. The council of State decided it in favor of the Duke of *Guife,* becaufe the prefence of the peers of France, who are twelve in number, fix ecclefiaftical and fix laical, was neceffary in this ceremony; whereas, the Princes of the blood, who have no function to difcharge in it, may difpenfe with their attendance. This light fpark ferved to inkindle and embitter more and more, the fpirits of all parties. The Admiral and Prince of *Conde* had fet every machine in motion to draw in the Conftable to their intereft: They were powerfully feconded by the Marfhal of *Montmorenci,* his eldeft fon, who was ftrictly connected with them. The Conftable, always firm in his refolutions, could not determine to difhonor his old age, by placing himfelf at the head of a party, nor by leagueing himfelf with thofe whom he thought new enemies of religion. The Admiral, always fruitful in refources and expedients, imagined one at this time, calculated to bring the Conftable into their views, by ways more indirect. There was then held at Pontoife, an affembly of fome deputies of the Provinces, to deliberate

deliberate upon the means of acquitting the immenfe debts, which the crown had contracted in
the laft wars. The Marfhal of *Montmorenci* pre-
fided in it. There were alfo fome friends of the
Admiral. He made ufe of them, to bring upon
the carpet, whatever he thought proper. The
Colignies and the Prince of *Conde*, there demanded, by the organ of their confidents, that they
fhould oblige all thofe who had received benefits
or gratifications, from the Kings Francis Ift and
Henry IId, to report them to the royal treafury,
pretending, that a calculation being made, without impofing now burthens, they might extinguifh the greateft part of the debt, which both
within and without the kingdom, crufhed the
ftate and individuals.

Thofe who had received the greateft benefac-
tions from the late Kings, were the *Guifes, Diana*
of Valentinois, the Marfhal *Saint Andre,* and the
Conftable. They were defirous indeed of hum-
bling the former : but as to the latter, they
meant only to infpire him with fears and jealoufies, and to force him to join the party of the
Princes ; that he might not expofe himfelf to
lofe the fruit of fo many years of fervices and
toils. The animofity of faction was fo lively, that
the *Colignies* were not afraid to excite in their
uncle thofe chagrins and inquietudes. But this
ftep had the ordinary fortune of defigns too
fubtle and too refined. It produced an effect directly contrary to that which was intended. The
propofition amounted to nothing lefs, than to
take away from the Conftable and the *Guifes,* the
greateft part of their property. *Diana,* of Valentinois, with whom both parties had formed
alliances, began to fecond the Conftable, concerning

ing this refearch, which interefted them equally.
She concerted her plan with art, or a kind of
prudence, which is not uncommon in women of
her character ; her averfion for the Queen, and
her fears of lofing all the gains of her trade,
made her think that the true means of her fafety, would be to allure the Conftable into the
party of the Catholic religion, and a clofer connection with the *Guifes*.   She launched out into
invectives againft the Admiral and the Prince of
Conde, whom fhe confidered as the authors of the
propofition made at the affembly at Pontoife ;
fhe deplored the miferies of the ftate, whofe
government, in the hands of a child and a foreign woman, was the inftrument of pernicious
councils, to foment the ambition and gratify the
paffions of certain individuals, to whom were
facrificed the fafety and tranquility of the kingdom ; into which they introduced, without
fhame, herefies condemned by the Church, and
againft which the late Kings, with juft feverity,
had employed fire and fword.   She added, with
the fame vivacity, and fincerity, that all France
was aftonifhed and enraged, to fee, that a *Montmorenci*, whofe houfe had been the firft of the
whole nation to embrace Chriftianity ; that a
man, who for fo long a time had filled the firft
office in the ftate, fhould at prefent allow himfelf to be fafcinated by the artifices of a woman ;
and that, a flave to her caprices, and to the imperfect information of the King of Navarre, he
confented to all their enterprizes againft religion.
She remonftrated to the Conftable, that having
the arms and the power in his hands, he was in-
difpenfibly obliged to oppofe the pernicious defigns of government, and to watch ftill, as he
had

had done fo many times before, over the confervation of a tottering throne, and a religion
wholly forfaken. She recalled to his recollection
that ancient conduct which had procured him fo
much glory, in oppofing the aggrandizement of
ftrangers. She conjured him that he would not
fuffer two women, one an Italian, the other of
Navarre, to ruin the principal foundations of the
French Monarchy; that is to fay, religion and
piety; to remember that the regent was the fame
Catharine, whofe conduct he had always cenfured, and whofe character he detefted; that the
Hugonots were thofe fame fectaries, whom he
had fo eagerly perfecuted under Henry IId; that
neither the perfons nor the nature of things were
changed; that the whole world would believe,
that enfeebled by age, he let himfelf be guided,
either by the ambition or caprice of others, fince
he appeared fo different from what he had been.
Such was the language of *Diana*, and who fo
proper as an harlot, to proftitute religion to the
purpofes of ambition, avarice, and faction. The
only wonder is, that thefe difcourfes of the
Dutchefs, which fhe took care frequently to re-
peat, began to make an impreffion on the Conftable. Sometimes an indignation againft his
nephews, fometimes the apprehenfions of lofing
his fortune, and fometimes his hatred againft
Calvinifm, fo difpofed him to liften to the Dutchefs, that at length her infinuations, together
with thofe of *Magdalen* of Savoy, his wife, fucceeded to detach him from the party of the
Queen. This *Magdalen* faw with vexation the
unbounded favors granted to the *Colignies*, which
fhe wifhed might be conferred on her brother
Honore, of Savoy, Marquis of Villars. Thus her
jealoufy

jealoufy neglected nothing to ferve the latter, and, to hurt the nephews of her hufband. *Diana* alfo, engaged the Marfhal *de Saint Andre* to fecond her in this negotiation. The fear of lofing his fortune, the violent hatred which he conceived againft the *Colignies*, and the plaufible pretext of preferving the Catholic faith, urged him to employ his influence with the Conftable in favor of the *Guifes ;* who, as foon as they were informed of it, omitted neither artifices, fubmiffions nor intrigues, to compleat the conqueft ; hoping by this means to re-eftablifh their power, or at leaft to recover a great part of it. The Marfhal of *Montmorenci* was the only one who could crofs this negotiation. But *Diana*, his wife, having fallen fick at Chantilly, he was obliged to leave his father, to attend her. The *Guifes*, difembarraffed of this obftacle, put the laft hand to their agreement with the Conftable, for the prefervation of the Catholic religion and the mutual defence of their fortunes.

The Queen informed of this union, thought herfelf deprived of her firmeft fupport, and dreaded, that the Princes of Lorrain, fupported by the credit of the Conftable, and difcontented with her, might attempt to take from her the regency. She thought it neceffary therefore, to connect herfelf more ftrictly with the King of Navarre, to counterbalance this new party. She directed all her cares to maintain that equilibrium, which affured her power, and that of her fon. She entered into all the views of the King of Navarre, in favor of the Hugonots. Under the pretext of maintaining peace during the minority of the King, and of conciliating the hearts of the people, by a reputation of clemency, fhe publifhed new

z   declarations,

declarations, which enjoined upon all the parliaments and all the other magiftrates of each province, to moleft no man on account of religion ;
to reftore the goods, houfes and poffeffions to
all thofe, who, in times paft, had been deprived of them, on fufpicion of herefy.   The parliament of Paris, and fome other magiftrates refufed to comply : but the Hugonots, thinking
themfelves authorized by the will and orders of
the King, of the regent, and the difpofitions of
the council, affumed to themfelves, as they had a
better right to do from God and nature, a liberty of confcience, and their numbers and forces
augmented from day to day.   This was to fulfil the views of the Queen, if thefe religionifts
had known how to reftrain themfelves within
the bounds of moderation and reafon.   But as
it commonly happens to people, who fuffer themfelves to be tranfported by their paffions, and
will not conform to the reftraints of authority :
as foon as they felt themfelves tolerated, protected, and delivered from the fear of punifhment,
their refentments of former ill ufage arofe, they
loft the refpect due to the magiftrates, and fometimes by public affemblies, and fometimes by injurious difcourfes, or other violent proceedings,
they drew upon themfelves the hatred and indignation of the Catholicks.   Hence arofe obftinate
difputes, which throwing the two parties into
quarrels, fpread tumult and infurrections thro
all the provinces of the kingdom.   Thus, contrary to the intentions of government, and the
expectations of the public, the remedy employed
to fave the ftate and maintain peace, became, at
leaft as our Hiftorian reprefents, contagious and
prejudicial; and occafioned precifely thofe trou-
                                            bles

bles and dangers, which they fought fo carefully to prevent.

The *Guifes*, we may be fure were not at all mortified at this turn of affairs. It was precifely what they wifhed. Encouraged and fortified by their union with the Conftable, they feized this occafion to oppofe the Queen and the King of Navarre. The Cardinal of Lorrain, finding the moment favorable to explaim himfelf in council, without regard to the Queen or the King of Navarre, who were prefent, began to fpeak on the ftate of religion, and to reprefent, with all the vehemence of his character, that it was to betray religion, and to difhonor themfelves in the eyes of the whole earth, to grant, in a moft chriftian kingdom, liberty of confcience, to innovators already condemned by councils and the voice of the church. That not fatisfied with diffeminating monftrous opinions, with corrupting the rifing generation, and impofing on the fimplicity of the weak, they blow up the fire of rebellion in all the provinces of the kingdom. That already the infolence and outrages of thefe Heretics, hindered the minifters of the church from celebrating mafs, and from appearing in their pulpits, and left to the magiftrates fcarce a fhadow of authority ; that every thing was a prey to the fword and flames, by the imprudence and obftinacy of thofe who arrogated to themfelves the licence of believing and teaching at their pleafure ; that the firft kingdom of Chriftendom was upon the point of making a fchifm, of fhaking off the yoke of obedience due to the holy fee, and of abandoning the Catholic faith, to fatisfy the caprice of an handful of feditious men. The Cardinal, enforced thefe arguments with fo much

much energy, with that confidence and natural eloquence which gave him such an afcendancy, even in the moft problematical opinions, that the protectors of the Hugonots oppofed nothing to him but filence. The King of Navarre and the Queen replied not a word, and even the Chancellor appeared amazed and confounded. The counfellors of ftate, irritated againft the Hugonots, were of opinion to affemble immediately all the Princes and officers of the crown, to the parliament of Paris, there to treat on this fubject, in the prefence of the King, and determine the means of curing thefe diforders. This affembly was accordingly held on the 13th of July, 1561, in parliament. The King of Navarre dared not alone to make oppofition openly ; this would have been to declare himfelf a Calvinift. The Queen indeed, defired that the Catholic party fhould not prevail ; but fhe was not the lefs apprehenfive that they would impute to her the eftablifhment and progrefs of Herefy. The contefts in parliament were however, animated : the partizans of the Hugonots, forgot nothing to procure them liberty of confcience, as the only means proper to appeafe all troubles, and heal all divifions. Their efforts were ufelefs. There was fome reafon for faying, that liberty of confcience was evidently oppofed to the fpirit and authority of the Catholic church ; but none at all for pretending that it was contrary to the fundamental laws of the kingdom.

It was decided that the Calviniftical preachers and minifters fhould be chafed out of the kingdom : and that they fhould conform in the public worfhip, only to the cuftoms and ceremonies authorized by the Roman church. All affemblies,

blies, of every kind and in every place, with arms or without, except in the Catholic churches, there to hear divine fervice, according to their ufages, were forbidden. To grant, however, fome mitigation to the Hugonots, they added in the fame Edict, that the cognizance of the crime of Herefy, fhould be referved to Bifhops and their grand Vicars; and if they had recourfe to the fecular arm, they could not condemn the guilty, but to banifhment; finally, they gave a general amnefty for all diforders committed in times paft, on account of religion. A declaration was drawn, figned by the King, the Queen, and all the Princes and lords of both parties.

The Prince of *Conde* and the Admiral, irritated to fee fuppreffed a party, upon whofe number and forces they had founded all their hopes, and not being able to hinder the execution of the Edict, which all the parliaments and moft of the inferior tribunals preffed into execution with great ardor, imagined another expedient; it was to engage the minifters of the Hugonots to demand a public conferrence, in prefence of the King, with the Catholic Prelates, upon the controverted points. This indirect method appeared to them proper to obtain infenfibly, a liberty of confcience. The Cardinal *de Tournon*, and feveral other Catholic Prelates, oppofed this requeft; they remonftrated that it was ufelefs to difpute about religion, with a people who were very obftinate, and who perfifted in a doctrine condemned by the church. That if they wifhed to lay open their reafons, they might addrefs themfelves to the council of Trent. The Cardinal of *Lorrain* was of opinion in favor of the conference; whether he flattered himfelf that he fhould con-
                                    found

found the Hugonots, by his irrefiftable reafoning, and convince thofe whom he thought feduced, or whether, as thofe who envied him gave out, by making an oftentatious exhibition of his eloquence and erudition, he wifhed ftill further to increafe his reputation and glory, in fo celebrated an affembly : Whatever were his intentions, it is certain that by not oppofing the demand of the Proteftants, he draws into his fentiment the prelates, who yielded to the folicitations of the King of Navarre. This Prince, who had long defired to hear a difpute in form, between the Catholics and Hugonots, to clear up his own doubts, fupported with warmth the demand of the Proteftants. They fent therefore fafe conducts to the minifters refugees at Geneva, and affigned for the place of conference Poify, a little city, five leagues from Paris.

The King appeared at Poify, with all his court, accompanied by the Cardinals of *Bourbon*, of *Lorrain*, of *Tournon*, of *Armagnac*, and of *Guife*, who were to affift at the conference on the part of the Catholics. The moft diftinguifhed Bifhops and Prelates, feveral Doctors of the Sorbonne, and other Theologians of the moft celebrated univerfities of the kingdom, were prefent. There appeared on the fide of the Hugonots, *Theodore Beza, Peter Martyr Vermilly, Francis de Saint Paul, John Raymond, John Virel*, with feveral others, who came from Geneva, or Germany. *Beza* explained his doctrines, with great pomp of eloquence ; and the Cardinal of *Lorrain* anfwered him, with what he called proofs and authorities, drawn from the Scriptures and the fathers of the Church. The council judged proper to withdraw the young King, becaufe the tendernefs of

his

his age not permitting him to difcern the truth, there was reafon to fear, that he might be fur-prized by fome dangerous opinion, contrary to the faith. After feveral debates, the affembly feparated without deciding any thing.

The Cotholics gained only one advantage. The King of Navarre was not fatisfied with the Hugonots, having obferved fome variations of their minifters in the doctrines which they main-tained. Some followed literally the fentiments of *Calvin;* others inclined to the doctrine of *Luther;* thefe adhered to the profeffion of faith of the Swifs, thofe to the confeffion of *Augfbourg.* Shocked with this inconfiftency, as he thought it, this weak Prince began to be difgufted with the new opinions, and to attach himfelf to the Catholic religion. But the Hugonots drew from this conference all the fruit that they had prom-ifed themfelves. As foon as they came out of it, they boafted highly that they had demonftrated the truth of their belief, convinced the Catholic doctors, confounded the Cardinal of *Lorrain,* and obtained of the King permiffion to preach their doctrine. In fact, of their own private authori-ty, they began to affemble, wherever they pleaf-ed, to hold publickly their fermons, with fo great an affluence of people, and fo great a concourfe of nobility, as well as others, that it was no long-er poffible to reftrain them.

When the magiftrates attempted to hinder their affemblies, or the Catholics attempted to chafe them from the churches where they met, the Hugonots run to arms, and defended them-felvts. The two parties attacked each other with fury, under the names of Hugonots and Papifts. The whole kingdom was in a flame.

The

The power of the magiftrates loft its energy;
the people were in continual terror and alarms;
the collection of the revenues was interrupted,
and in the bofom of peace, an inteftine and cruel
war was feen to be inkindled. The Queen-Mother and the King of Navarre, moved with thefe
exceffes, feeing that the feverity of the Edict of
July, had only increafed the diforders, convoked
another affembly of deputies from all the parliaments of the kingdom, to be informed by them,
of the ftate of each province, and to deliberate
upon the moft proper means of re-eftablifhing
tranquility. *The views of the miniftry changing
continually, as the interefts of minifters and the paffions
of the great varied; it was not aftonifhing, that
after fo many meafures taken, abandoned, reaffumed,
affairs fhould ftill remain in greater diforder, and a
more ftrange confufion* It was indeed impoffible
that fuch frequent variations fhould reftore good
order, which an equal and uniform conduct
could alone maintain.

This affembly was holden at Paris, in the beginning of the year 1562. The Queen, according to her ordinary maxims, employed herfelf in
holding the balance between the two parties, and
to hinder one from prevailing over the other,
for fear fhe fhould be the victim of the ftrongeft.
The greateft part of the magiftrates concurred in
her views; fome perfuaded that it was impoffible
to reftrain fo great a multitude, animated by a
furious zeal for religion, and others feeing with
regret fo much blood fhed to no good purpofe.
They prepared that famous Edict of January,
which granted to the Hugonots, the liberty of
confcience, and the liberty of holding their affemblies and preaching their fermons, upon condition
                                                          that

that they fhould meet without arms, without the cities, in the fields, and in prefence of the judges of the places. The parliaments and other tribunals oppofed, at firft, the execution of this Edict; but it was finally regiftered, upon repeated letters of juffion, (fealed commands to do a thing which they had refufed to do) of the King and Council. This was a thunder bolt to the chiefs of the Catholic party. To bring on a crifis, to force all the Catholics to join them, and to hinder the execution of the Edict, the Duke of *Guife*, the Conftable, all the Cardinals, except de *Tournon*, who was lately dead, the Marfhals *de Briffac* and *Saint Andre* quitted the court, to oppofe themfelves with all their forces to the Calviniftical party. So near was liberty of confcience at that time, to a compleat and final eftablifhment in France, that nothing but this violent meafure could have prevented it ; even this retreat of all the Catholics would not have fucceeded, without another artifice. They fufficiently forefaw, that as long as the good intelligence fubfifted between the Queen-mother and the King of Navarre, they fhould have no power to intermeddle in the government of the kingdom, and that all their efforts would be in vain ; they propofed therefore to break it. Convinced that the Queen-mother would never change her plan or her conduct, at leaft until the majority of her fon , they thought it would be more eafy to gain upon the underftanding of the king of Navarre. Their recefs enabled them to conduct with more fecrecy this negociation, which required time and addrefs. *D'Eft*, legate of the Pope, and *Manriquez* ambaffador of Spain, let into the fecret and entrufted

A a   with

with the conduct of it, eafily commenced the conferences, by the interpofition of the confidents of the King of Navarre. This weak Prince, had, or pretended to have, no longer the fame incli-nation for the Hugonots, fince the colloquy at Poiffy, where he had remarked their variations upon the contefted points of faith, and not hav-ing found in *Theodore Beza*, nor in *Peter Martyr*, the fame confidence as he thought, as they affect-ed when they dogmatized without contradictors, he had confulted Doctor *Baudouin*, equally verfed in fcriptures and in controverfy. This theolo-gian had decided the King of Navarre, to re-unite himfelf to the faith of the church, and to adopt neither the profeffion of faith of the Swifs Protef-tants, nor the confeffion of Augfbourg. His ac-quiefcence in the Edict of January was lefs from any inclination to the Hugonots, than from an opinion that confciences ought not to be reftrain-ed, and that toleration was an infallible means of extinguifhing the troubles of the kingdom. As foon as his confidents, already difpofed to ferve the Catholic party, had informed the legate and ambaffador, that he was in this temper, thefe laft failed not to take advantage of it, to open the negotiation. In order to unite to motives of confcience, perfonal advantages and temporal in-terefts, they propofed to him to divorce his Queen Jane, with a difpenfation from the Pope, becaufe fhe was an Heretic, and to marry Mary, Queen of Scots, the niece of the *Guifes*, and widow of Francis IId, a Princefs who united to the charms of youth and beauty, the actual poffeffion of a great kingdom. The King of Navarre, attached to his children, rejected firmly this propofition. They then brought upon the carpet, once more, the

the exchange of Sardinia, fo often propofed in
vain. This was the delicate point. which touched him the moft fenfibly. His hopes indeed,
were not very ftrong; but this negotiation not
having been wholly broken off, *Manriquez*, the
Spanifh ambaffador, by his ordinary artifice, renewed it with fo much apparent ferioufnefs, as
to re-animate the defires and the confidence of
the King of Navarre. Not content with giving
him the ftrongeft affurances of the good difpofitions of the Catholic King, he proceeded fo far
as to treat of the means of exchange, and of the
quality of the rents and fervices, which the King
of Navarre fhould render the crown of Spain,
as acknowledgments of its fovereignty. They
debated thefe claufes and conditions as ferioufly,
as if they were upon the point of figning the
treaty. The character of the King of Navarre,
and his inclination to embrace always the moft
honorable and plaufible meafures, favored the
defigns of the Catholics.

This Prince (the King of Navarre,) began
gravely to acknowledge that the Hugonots difguifed their paffions and their interefts, under
the veil of chriftian charity, and the cloak of religion. Moreover, he was made to apprehend
that the Admiral, with his policy, would perfuade all France to believe that the King of Navarre followed blindly his councils. They piqued
his jealoufy, by reprefenting to him that the
Calvinifts highly blamed his floth and indolence,
while all their affections and attachments were to
the Prince of *Conde*, whofe courage, promptitude,
and magnanimity, they never ceafed to exalt and
celebrate. A laft confideration of extreme importance, touched a nerve of exquifite fenfibility :
The

The King of France and his brothers were of feeble and delicate complexions, ill conftituted, fubject to dangerous diftempers, and too young to have children. The fucceffion to the crown, regarded him as the firft Prince of the blood, and to declare himfelf the head and protector of the Hugonots, was to place between the throne and him, an impenetrable barrier. To fmooth his way the more eafily to the throne, he inclined to re-unite himfelf to the Catholic party, to attract the favor of the Pope and the King of Spain, and to attach to himfelf the forces of the faction, which was the beft united, and the moft powerful. He began to diftruft the councils of the Queen his wife, blindly devoted to Calvinifm, and naturally an enemy of pacific meafures. The magnificent promifes and perfuafive difcourfes of the legáte, and of *Manriquez*, joined to fo many other motives, determined him finally to unite himfelf with the Conftable and the Duke of *Guife*. They declared loudly in words and by writings, that they were leagued only for the defence of the Catholic religion ; but their views were, in reality, much more vaft. The King of Navarre abandoned one party, in which he found himfelf eclipfed by his brother, to attach himfelf to another, in which they offered him more brilliant hopes. And the *Guifes* entered into this convention, only to re-eftablifh their credit and ancient grandeur.

Such was the union, which taught the French the art of forming leagues and combinations, without the knowledge of their fovereigns. The Hugonots reprefented it in the moft odious colours, and called it the triumvirate. The Queen Jane conceived a lively refentment of this unexpected

pected refolution of her hufband. Full of indignation to fee him become the moft ardent perfe-
cutor of her favorite religion, in which fhe flattered herfelf fhe had confirmed him ; fhe refolved to quit the court, and retired into Bearn, with
the Prince Henry, and the Princefs Catharine,
her children, whom fhe inftructed in the reformed religion, declining all further fociety, and
commerce with her hufband. The Queen-mother
was not lefs alarmed with a change fo fudden
and incredible. *The triumvirate deftroyed all the
projects of an equilibrium, which fhe had founded, on
the diftrufts and animofities which divided the grandees.* She dreaded as much, for the fafety of her
children, as for her own authority. Thefe reciprocal variations, thefe combinations of interefts,
totally oppofite to each other, announced clearly
enough to her underftanding, that this union
concealed high hopes, and vaft defigns. She
knew that the *Guifes* had unravelled her artifices,
and that burning with ambition, they fought
every' means of re-entering into the miniftry.
Moreover, what probability was there, that the
King of Navarre would renounce the friendfhip
of his brother, and of his moft faithful partizans,
to unite with his moft cruel enemies, if he had
not been affured of great advantages in fuch a
change. She was not ignorant of the empire
which is held over human hearts, even the moft
upright, by ambition and the thirft of ruling.
Finally, confidering every thing which threatened
her, fhe could not diffemble her own weaknefs,
nor that of her children. Forced by thefe reflections to truft no longer, either the fincerity
of the King of Navarre, nor the demonftrations
made by the Catholics, of having no-defign of
making

making any innovation in the government; a prey to conftant terrors, alarms and fufpicions, nothing was capable. of calming her inquietude. She paffed often whole nights, in conference with her confidents, and among others with the Bifhop of *Valance*, and the Chancellor *De L'Hopital :* Their counfels, and above all, the critical pofition in which fhe ftood, determined her to form a coalition with the Prince of *Conde* and the Admiral, to favor their defigns, and fupport herfelf with their forces, in order to counterbalance, as much as poffible, the power of the oppofite faction : alledging among other motives, to her Catholic confidents, that God himfelf permits evil for the fake of good : and fince the Hugonots had caufed fo many diforders, it was but juft to make ufe of them, to cure the diftempers which had infected the heart of the ftate.

The Hugonots delivered from the fear of punifhment, by the publication of the Edict of January, had began to recover courage, and held frequently public affemblies ; their party appeared confiderable, both by their number and the quality of their members : and their forces were not inconfiderable. The Prince of Conde had openly declared himfelf their head ; he was, in appearance, reconciled with the Guifes, in obedience to the orders of the King : but, in his heart he burnt with an impatient defire to revenge himfelf, againft his principal perfecutors, for the outrages which he had received. The Admiral, who in the view to aggrandize himfelf, as well as his brothers, more ftrictly united than ever to the party of the Hugonots, moderated the ardor and vehemence of the Prince, by the maturity of his counfels. Under thefe chiefs,

and

and in the fame fentiments, were engaged the Prince of *Porcien*, the Lords of *Genlis*, of *Grammont*, of *Duras*, the Earls of *Rochefoucault* and of *Montgomery*, the Barons of *Ardrets*, of *Bonchavannes*, *Soubire*, and feveral other great men of the kingdom. With any, the leaft authority of government, they were in a condition to refift, and oppofe boldly the oppofite party.

The Queen, forced as fhe thought to take advantage of a conjuncture fo favorable for her own defence, and that of her children ; and reduced to the neceffity of embracing the firft party which prefented, however dangerous it might be, expected from time and events, the unravelling all their intrigue. She feigned to be ftaggered by the reafonings of the Hugonots, and difpofed to embrace their opinions. To confirm them fhe was more in this opinion, by exterior demonftrations, fhe caufed their minifters to come into her apartment, and appeared to hear them with pleafure. She manifefted great confidence and benevolence to the Admiral, and the Prince of *Conde*, in the frequent converfations fhe had with them. She deceived the Dutchefs of *Montpenfier*, by her falfe confidences, and made ufe of her, to allure the principal Hugonots ; the better to color the promifes and hopes, which fhe gave in fecret, by apparent meafures. She wrote even to the Pope in equivocal terms. Sometimes fhe demanded a free and general council, fuch as the Calvinifts defired : fometimes, permiffion to convoke a national council. Another time fhe folicited the ufe of the communion in both kinds, a difpenfation to priefts to marry; the liberty of praying in the vulgar language, and other fimilar innovations, as the Catholics called

called them, which the Hugonots wished, and introduced. *De Lisle*, the French ambassador at Rome, seconded her so perfectly, that, by exciting doubts concerning her faith in the minds of the Pope and the Catholics, she obliged them to observe great caution in their own conduct, for fear they should irritate her, and disgust her against the Roman religion. By the same artifice she deceived the penetration, and gained the hearts of the Hugonots, by persuading them that she was wholly disposed in their favor : to such a degree, that the implacable hatred which they once bore her, had given place to confidence and attachment. It was not only the people that she amused by these appearances : the Admiral himself, in spight of all his appearance, policy and penetration, had suffered himself to be seduced. He hesitated not to give the Queen a circumstancial account of the number, forces and designs of the Calvinists, of the correspondences which they maintained, both within and without the kingdom, and of all other particulars which concerned his party ; as soon as she gave him to understand, that she desired to have exact information before she declared herself, assuring him that she would embrace openly that party, as soon as it should be sufficiently powerful to place her out of the reach of the vengeance of the Catholics and the triumvirate, composed of the Duke of *Guise*, the Constable and the King of Navarre. Thus, by a change equally prompt and incredible, the King of Navarre attached himself to the Catholic party, and Queen Catharine, at least in appearance, became favorable to the Hugonots. These variations were at the time attributed to the levity of mind of the King of Navarre, and the

the natural inconftancy of the fex of the Queen : and it is thus that fome Hiftorians have fince judged, who were either not capable, or had not opportunity, like *Davila*, to unravel the fecret fprings of thefe refolutions.

Is it poffible to place an unbalanced government, in a light more defpicable or more contemptible ! Can human nature be more difgraced, than by this endlefs feries of unions, feparations, coalitions, combinations and tergiverfations? And yet it is moft obvious, that fuch a feries muft forever be the effect of a conftitution, where there is no legal equilibrium.

No. 24.

AFFAIRS had now taken a new face. It was eafy to forefee, that the animofities of the two factions would never be extinguifhed but by arms—and that the tempeft which had long grumbled in the air, would foon pour upon their heads. Accident foon produced a favorable conjuncture for precipitating France into the greateft misfortunes. The King of Navarre, having declared himfelf openly for the Catholic party, fixed his refidence at Paris. This city, fituated in the centre of France, is much more populous, more rich, more magnificent and more powerful, than any other in the kingdom. This Prince, believing that the other cities would eafily conform to the example of the capital, forgot nothing to

B b   hinder

hinder the Hugonots from holding their affemblies, and preaching their fermons there; in
which the Parifians in general, enemies of the
reformation, feconded him with zeal. By this
means he hoped in time to diminifh infenfibly
the credit and the forces of the Proteftants, and
take away their liberty of confcience, which a-
lone fupported their exiftence. The Prince of
Conde refided alfo at Paris, where he promoted
and fomented the defigns of the Hugonot minifters. Under the pretext of caufing to be obferved the edict of January, he extended from day
to day the liberty of confcience ; and, whether
by power or by right, arrogated to himfelf a
great authority in what refpected the State. The
King of Navarre, animated equally againft his
brother by a love of repofe, and by jealoufy, refolved to compel him to go out of Paris. Several
other motives determined him to put an end to
troubles and feditions, as well as conventicles, in
a city which was the firmeft fupport of the
Catholic party ; but whether he felt himfelf too
weak to attempt fuch an enterprize alone, or
whether he wifhed to confult his confederates
before he executed any thing, he invited the
Duke of Guife and the Conftable to come and
join him, with their partifans.

The Duke of Guife, fince his retirement from
Court, refided at Joinville, one of his country
feats, upon the frontiers of Champaine and Picardy. Upon the invitation of the King of Navarre, he departed for Paris, accompanied by the
Cardinal his brother, a numerous retinue of gentlemen attached to his interefts, and two companies of men in arms. The firft of March, in the
morning, as he paffed by Vaffi, a little city in
Champaine,

Champaine, his people heard an unufual ringing of bells, and having afked the reafon of it, were told that it was the fignal of a fermon at which the Hugonots affembled. The valets and footmen of the Duke, who were moft forward on the road, excited by the fingularity of the thing, and by curiofity to fee one of thefe affemblies, which were but lately begun to be holden publicly, advanced in a tumult, uttering their coarfe jokes, towards the place where the Hugonots were affembled to hear their minifters. The Calvinifts underftanding that the Duke of Guife, whom they regarded as one of their moft ardent perfecutors, was not far off, and feeing a troop of his people coming directly to them, whether they dreaded fome infult, or whether they were piqued at the rude raileries and fcornful fpeeches of this fervile mob, they anfwered by acts of violence, pelting with ftones the firft who were advancing towards their congregation.

This is the account of Davila—and at this day it may be of as little confequence to enquire which fide began to ufe force, as to afertain which party fired the firft gun at our Lexington. When a nation is prepared for a civil war, when parties are formed and paffions enflamed, which can be extinguifhed no other way, it is only for the fake of popularity, neceffary to enquire which ftrikes the firft blow. But in our American revolution, we know it was the party who were in the habit of domineering who began—and fuch is commonly the cafe. Moft probably De Thou is in the right, for the fame reafon—who afferts, that the Duke of Guife's fervants threw the firft ftones; and if this was done without the Duke's orders, it is certain that his mother, a bigotted a bigotted furious Catholic, had often entreated him to deliver her from the neighbourhood of the Proteſtants of Vaſſi; and very probably ſhe had enflamed his whole family againſt them. However this might be, the Catholics abandoned all their prudence and attacked the Proteſtants, ſword in hand, and the ſkirmiſh ſoon become furious. The Duke, informed of the tumult, and wiſhing to appeaſe it, ran in all haſte and ruſhed into the midſt of the cambatants—while he repremanded his own people, and exhorted the Hugonots to retire, he was ſlightly wounded by the ſtroke of a ſtone upon his left jaw. The blood which he loſt obliged him to retire from the uproar, when his followers, growing outrageous, had recourſe to fire-arms, forced the houſe where the Calviniſts had barricadoed themſelves, killed more than ſixty of them; and their miniſter, dangerouſly wounded, eſcaped with great difficulty over the roofs of the neighbouring houſes. When the commotion was aſſuaged, the Duke of Guiſe ſent for the Judge of the place, and reprimanded him for tolerating ſuch conventicles. The Judge excuſed himſelf, becauſe theſe aſſemblies were permitted by the edict of January. The Duke, as much enraged at this anſwer as at the diſorder which occaſioned it, laid his hand on the hilt of his ſword, and replied, with great fury, "The edge of this iron ſhall ſoon deliver us from the edict which they think ſo ſolidly eſtabliſhed." Theſe words, uttered in the ardor of his indignation, did not eſcape the attention of thoſe who heard them—and in the ſequel he was accuſed of being the Boute-feu, and the author of the civil wars.

The Hugonots, irritated by the maſſacre at Vaſſi, could

could no longer contain themfelves within the bounds of moderation—not content with the exceſſes committed by them in feveral cities of the kingdom, and efpecially in Paris, where they had maſſacred feveral Catholics, and fet fire to the church of St. Medard; they liſtened only to their own rage, and excited every where troubles and bloody feditions; monaſteries were pillaged, images broken, altars overturned, and churches profaned. Theſe exceſſes, on both fides, embittered mens' minds, and they ruſhed every where to arms. The chiefs of the two parties, agitated by the fame motives, aſſembled their forces and prepared openly for war. But the leaders of both factions were not ignorant that, in the actual ſtate of things, they could not take arms without rendering themfelves guilty of rebellion, and that there was neither pretext nor colour which could authorife any meafures which tended to war. The Catholics could not interrupt the execution of the edict of January, without controverting openly the decifions of the council, and wounding the royal authority from which this edict had iſſued. The Hugonots had no reafonable motive to revolt, while they were protected and allowed to enjoy the liberty of confcience granted them by that edict. The leaders of each party defired *to draw the King to their fide, and to become maſters of his perfon*, either to abolifh the edict, or to derive new advantages from it, in order to prove that their caufe was the moſt juſt—and that it was the oppofite party which erected the ſtandard of revolt, by oppofing the apparent will of the Sovereign, and by attacking even his perfon.

No.

No. 25.

THE Queen, perfectly informed of all these projects, and wishing to preserve, with all her power, her own liberty and that of her children, continued to play off her artifices, to balance the power of the Grandees, and to prevent the ascendency of one party over the other, from drawing after it, the ruin of the State. Thus, that she might not be obliged to favor, one or the other party, she quitted Paris and retired to Fontainbleau. She thought that in this residence, where she was more at liberty, that in Paris, they could not compel her to declare herself, and she still studied to support her confidence, which she had managed with both factions, whose Chiefs she amused by equivocal discourses, and ambiguous promises. The Prince of Condé, and Coligni, yielding to the superiority of the Catholic party, had quitted Paris, to take arms. The Queen gave them secretly to understand, that she was disposed to join them, as soon as she should see them supported by forces sufficient to make head against their enemies. On the other hand, she protested to the King of Navarre, the Constable and the Duke of Guise, that she had no intention to separate herself from the Catholics, nor to consent to the new reform, any further than necessity and the advice of good men should oblige her, to grant to the Hugonots, a moderate liberty.

Her letters were not less ambiguous, than her words : and she did not explain herself more clearly abroad than at home. She gave continually

ually new inftructions to the ambaffadors in foreign courts, and efpecially to Delile, who refided at Rome. Sometimes fhe contracted and at other times fhe extended their powers ; and by thefe variations held all minds in fufpence. But this conduct began to be more delicate than ever. The Chiefs of the two parties. were not lefs politicians than herfelf : During the courfe of her regency they had found opportunities to unravel all her artifices, and penetrate all her difguifes. The King advanced in age, and that circumftance was to them a neceflity to haften the execution of their defigns. His minority might give to certain meafures a colour, which would no longer exift, when he would be of age ; when all ought to depend upon his will, to which they could no longer oppofe themfelves, without the guilt of rebellion : At the prefent moment they could pretend, that their oppofition was only to a bad adminiftration, and the pernicious defigns of thofe who governed under his authority.

Already the Duke of Guife, more enterprifing and more alive than the others, directed, at his pleafure, the refolutions of his party. He had drawn into his fentiments the Conftable and the King of Navarre, by perfuading them, that if they would all refort to court, *they might bring off the King and the Queen-Mother to the capital,* and reduce them to the neceflity of taking meafures, and iffuing edicts, as the Catholics fhould judge convenient to their interefts, without expofing themfelves, any longer, to the danger of being anticipated, and without permitting their enemies to feize on the King and avail themfelves of his authority. The Prince of Condé had formed the fame defign : He had retired at firft

to Meaux, and from thence to his eftate, at la
Ferté where he intended to affemble the main
body of his forces. This refolution was the effect
of the advice of the Admiral, fuggefted by the
Queen, and the projects of the Catholics, which
had not efcaped his penetration—nothing being
more common in civil wars, than to difcover the
defigns of the enemy either by the infidelity of
fome to the fecret, or by the multitude of fpies
who are employed. The chiefs of the Catholic
party had occafion only for their ordinary retinue to execute their defign ; the neighbourhood
of Paris, which was wholly devoted to them,
affured them of fufficient forces, and offered them
favorable opportunities. On the contrary, the
Prince of Condé, weaker than his enemies, and
followed by few troops, was obliged to wait for
the Lords of his party, and the nobility whom he
had fummoned from feveral provinces, who affembled but flowly. Thus the Catholics were
before-hand, by appearing all well attended at the
Court.

Their unforefeen arrival difconcerted not the
Queen. Although fhe depended little on the
fuccefs of her intrigues, fhe exerted herfelf to
perfuade the King of Navarre to depart from
Court, with the Princes and Lords who had accompanied him. " No man is ignorant," faid
fhe to him, " that the Catholic Lords would
take advantage of my weaknefs, and that of my
fon, to compel us, to regulate the State, according to their inclinations, by governing at the will
of their ambition and private interefts. This
conduct, directly oppofite to the principles of
honour and of fidelity, of which they boaft, is
not lefs contrary to the tranquility and the con-
                                        fervation

fervation of the State, which they pretend to
have alone in view. "To iffue new edicts, and
revoke thofe which have been publifhed, is it not
to put arms into the hands of the Hugonots?
Thefe fectaries, already fo audacious and fo ready
to revolt, will complain aloud of injuftice, if we
annul, without reafon, an edict prepared and accepted with the confent of both parties. During
the minority of the King, we ought to avoid war,
and the troubles infeparable from it, to the ut-
moft of our care and power. To whom will the
nation impute the difafters which will overwhelm
it? Will not an eternal infamy be the portion of
thofe who have the principal fhare in government? It was to avoid thefe dangers, and to take
away all pretexts from the incendiaries, that I
fubfcribed to the edict of January, and quitted
the capital. The moft effectual means of irritating
the violence of an evil, which as yet is only creep-
ing on fecretly, would be to carry us into a fufpected city, and repeal an edict already publifhed.
The King of Navarre, and the Catholic Princes,
ought to remember, that it belongs only to the
flagitious, whofe fortune is uncertain or defperate,
to excite civil wars. The Prince commands
without contradiction. The Lords of his party,
loaded with riches, dignities, employments and
honors, enjoy the moft flourifhing fortune. Can
they envy the people an imaginary and momentary liberty? Let them fuffer the King to arrive
at his majority, without feeing his kingdom dif-
tracted with war. Forced by neceffity, I have
only pardoned faults, which I could not punifh—
nor have I granted to the Hugonots other liberty
than that which they had ufurped. It is only by
management that we can cure the people of this

c c   phrenzy.

phrenzy. Let the Catholic Chiefs then arm themfelves with patience, for fear that, by rafh remedies, they may envenom an evil which may draw after it fatal revolutions, and the moft melancholly events. If however you are refolved to make any alteration in the edict, it ought only to be done by infenfible degrees, and by the favor of fuitable opportunities and conjunctures. To employ violent means, would be to furnifh the feditious with pretexts, which they feek with fo much ardour."

No. 26.

THESE reafons of the Queen, urged and re-peated with energy, would have ftaggered the King of Navarre, and perhaps the Conftable, if the Duke of Guife would have liftened to them. But he wifhed for war—by the favor of which he flattered himfelf, he fhould recover and even increafe his ancient power. Moreover, in quality of Chief, and Protector of the Catholic party, he wifhed to annul, by any means whatever, all that had been done againft his inclination, to the prejudice of the Church—and to arrogate to himfelf all the glory of fuch a revolution. He combatted therefore, with vivacity, all the rea-fons of the Queen, and remonftrated to his con-federates, that they would infallibly lofe all their credit and reputation, by fuffering themfelves to be fo eafily amufed by a woman, who had no other

other defign than to throw herfelf into the arms of the oppofite party as foon as they, from a blind confidence in her words, fhould depart from Court. " Nothing" added the Duke, " will be more prejudicial to our caufe, nor more infa- mous for us, than to avow that it is neither the public good, nor the maintenance of the Royal Authority, but private paffions and perfonal in- terefts, which have put us in motion. It will be believed, that the remorfe of our confciences, has obftructed us, in the purfuit of our enterprife. The artificial difcourfes of the Queen, ought not to prevail with us, to abandon a refolution, ma- turely weighed, and taken by concert, nor to in- terrupt the execution of a project, dictated by rea- fon, prefcribed by honor, and commanded by that attachment, which we have profeffed to religion whofe prefervation and intereft, have chiefly de- termined us to this meafure. It is no longer the feafon to delay, and to wafte time in difputes. Already the Prince of Condé is advancing in arms—the forces of the Hugonots are affem- bled—they are ready *to feize on the perfon of the King, if we do not haften to place him in a fituation of fafety—and fince we cannot terminate this affair by perfuafion, let us not be intimidated from employing force : Let us take away the King,* and leave the Queen to take the part which fhe fhall judge moft convenient. The refolutions of this Prin- cefs are of little moment to us, as foon as we fhall be fupported by the prefence of our lawful Sovereign, aided by the authority of the firft Prince of the blood, to whom, by right of birth belongs the government of the kingdom."

The Prince of Condé, united with the Colignis and other Lords of his party, approached the
Court.

Court. The Conftable, and the King of Navaire, perfuaded by the Duke of Guife, gave the Queen to underftand, that it was neceffary to take her refolution, without lofs of time ; that for themfelves, they had refolved to conduct to Paris, the King and his brothers, for fear they fhould fall into the hands of the Hugonots, who, according to intelligence, were not far diftant. That they would not abandon their mafter to the mercy of hereticks, who intended to take him away, in order to make an ill ufe of his name, and undermine the foundations of the monarchy. That there was no time to be loft, or trifled away.— *That they fhould conduct the King to Paris, as their own honor, and the good of the ftate required :* That as to herfelf, they pretended not to conftrain her in any thing ; but fhould leave her, with all the refpect that was due to her, at liberty to difpofe of her perfon, as fhe fhould think fit. The Queen was not aftonifhed at this declaration, bold and fudden as it was. She had forefeen it, and determined, beforehand, on her plan, in fuch a fituation. Forced to declare herfelf, altho fhe forefaw that the two parties would foon come to blows, fhe would not abandon the Catholic party. She pretended that her honor, and her reafon, attached her to it : She imagined fhe faw her fafety, and that of her children in it. Taking therefore in an inftant her refolution, fhe anfwered, with her ufual prefence of mind, that no perfon was more attached than herfelf to the Catholic religion, nor more zealous for the good of the State—That fhe would, upon this occafion, give way to their fentiments—and fince they were all for quitting Fontainbleau, fhe would concur with them.

With

With the utmeſt promptitude ſhe gave orders for their departure; but at the ſame time ſhe wrote to the Prince of Condé a letter, in which ſhe lamented, that ſhe could not commit herſelf, and the perſon of the King, into the hands of his partizans, according to the promiſe ſhe had made him : That the Catholics had prevented them, by conducting them by force to Paris : That, provided he did not loſe his courage, ſhe exhorted him not to ſuffer his enemies to take poſſeſſion of the whole authority of government. She then commenced her journey, with the King and her other children, ſurrounded by the Triumvirate, and the other Catholic Lords, who to conſole her, treated her with great reſpect and honor. She arrived that evening at Melun, the next day at Vincennes, and in the morning of the third day at Paris. Many perſons obſerved the young King in tears, thinking the Catholic Lords had deprived him of his liberty. The Queen, irritated by the ill-ſucceſs of her artifices, and foreſeeing the calamities of an inevitable war, diſcovered, during the whole journey, a mournful and mortified air and countenance. The Duke of Guiſe was ſo little affected with this, that he ſaid freely and openly, that the *public good was a public good, whether it was obtained by conſent or by force.*

The Prince of Condé was informed, upon his march, of the departure of the King, and perceiving himſelf either prevented by the Catholics, or deceived by the Queen, made a halt, and remained ſome time undecided, what courſe he ſhould take. The terrible picture of thoſe dangers which threatened him, preſented itſelf in lively colours before his eyes ; but the Admiral, who had

had remained a little in the rear, arriving, they conferred together a few minutes, and the Prince, with a profound figh cried out, " The die is caft, we are too far advanced to retreat." He took immediately another road, and marched with rapidity towards Orleans, of which, he had for' fometime refolved to take poffeffion. This city, one of the principal of the Kingdom, about thirty leagues from Paris, is vaft, well built, and very populous ; it is fituated in the province of Beauce almoft in the middle of France upon the banks of the Loire, a large navigable river, which after having watered feveral provinces, falls into the ocean in Brittany. Orleans, by its navigation, and its facility of communication with feveral other provinces, appeared to the Prince very proper for a place of arms and the center of his party, and to be oppofed in fome fort, to Paris.

For feveral months, that he had meditated to make himfelf mafter of this city, he had entertained a fecret intelligence with fome of the inhabitants, inclined to the doctrines of Calvin, whom he employed to engage a great part of the young men, who were reftlefs, feditious and greedy of novelties. As it is not intended to relate in detail, the whole of this hiftory, it is fufficient to fay, that he got poffeffion of Orleans, that the two parties publifhed manifeftos, and that chicanery, negociations, battles, fieges, conflagrations and affaffinations, fucceeded in all their ufual train of horrors in civil wars.

No.

No. 27.

WE fhall now content ourfelves with reciting
the fummary of this firft civil war. After the
publication of declarations and manifeftoes, the
two armies took the field. The Queen-mother
wifhes to avoid a war, and procure peace : She
negociates an interview for this purpofe with the
Prince of Condé, but without fuccefs : She continues however to negociate an accommodation,
and obtains a conclufion of it. The Prince re-
pents of it, by the perfuafion of his partizans,
and refumes his arms. He attempts in the
night to furprize the royal army : His enterprize
fucceeds not. The King receives powerful rein-
forcements from Germany and Switzerland.
The Prince of Condé is obliged to fhut himfelf
up in Orleans, and feparate his army, which he
could not hold together in a body. He fends to
demand fuccours in Germany and England, and
confents to deliver Havre de Grace to the Englifh, and receive their garrifons into Rouen and
Dieppe. The Queen, irritated and afflicted at
thefe refolutions, joins the Catholic party, and
declares the Hugonots, rebels. The royal army
takes Blois, Tours, Poitiers, and Bourges. The
15th of Sept. 1562, it lays fiege to Rouen—in the
courfe of which, the King of Navarre, vifiting
the trenches to reconnoitre the ftate of the
place, was wounded in the left fhoulder, by a fhot
of an Arquebufe, which broke the bone, wounded the nerves, and felled him to the ground as if
he was dead. He was carried immediately to his
quarters,

quarters, where all the other generals assembled. The surgeons who dressed his wounds, in the presence of the King and Queen, judged it mortal, because the ball had penetrated too far, into the body.

The 26th of October 1562, the city was carried by assault, and the whole army entered, making a horrible carnage of the garrison and inhabitants, by putting to the sword, without any quarter, all who presented themselves armed or unarmed : The city was delivered up to be plundered, except the churches and consecrated things, which the soldiers were made to respect, by the vigilance and good discipline of the generals.

The King of Navarre, suffering under the pains of his wound, and wounded in spirit almost as much as in. body, insisted on embarking on the Seine, to be transported to Saint Maur, a pleasure-house near Paris, where he often went to take the air, and enjoy the tranquility of solitude. He scarce arrived at Andeli, a few leagues from Rouen, when his fever was augmented by the agitation of the batteau, he lost his senses, and died in a few hours. He united to his high birth, an elegant person, and a softness of manners : If he had lived in other times, and under a better constitution of government, he might have been reckoned among the greatest Princes of his age ; but the candor and sincerity of his heart, the sweetness and affability of his disposition, in the midst of political troubles, and civil dissentions, served only to hold him in continual agitation and inquietude. Inconstant in his projects, and uncertain in his resolutions—drawn away on one side by the impetuous character of his brother, and excited by the party of the Calvinists,

vinifts, in which he long held the firft rank—reftrained on the other hand by motives of honor,
as he thought, by his natural inclination for
peace, and averfion for civil wars, he difcovered
on many occafions but little firmnefs or conftancy
in his defigns. Placed in the number of thofe,
who lay under the reputation of feeking to difturb the ftate, he fhared in their difgrace—and
he was feen afterwards, at the head of the oppofite party, perfecuting thofe, whom he had formerly protected. In point of religion, fometimes
allured to Calvinifm, by the perfuafions of his
wife, and the difcourfes of Theodore Beza—and
fometimes brought back to the Catholic faith, by
the torrent of fafhion, and the eloquence of the
Cardinal of Lorraine, he gained the confidence
of neither party, and left in his dying moments,
fufpicious and equivocal ideas of his creed. Many thought, that, though he was in his heart
attached to Calvinifm, or rather to the confeffion
of Augfburg, he feparated from the Hugonots
from fecret views of ambition—and fuffering im-
patiently that the Prince his brother, by his valor
and greatnefs of foul had acquired among them
more efteem than himfelf, he chofe rather to
hold the firft rank among the Catholics than the
fecond among the Calvinifts. He died at the age
of forty-two, in a time when his prudence, increafing with age, he might perhaps have fur-
paffed the opinion which had been conceived of
him. Jane of Albret, his widow, continued in
poffeffion of the title of Queen, and of what remained of Navarre. She had two children, Henry, Prince of Bearn, then nine years of age, and
afterwards the all-glorious Henry the Fourth of
France, and the Princefs Catharine, then very

D d   young.

young. Their mother lived with them at Pau and at Nerac, fupervifing their education in the new religion.

The Prince of Conde, reinforced by the auxiliary forces from Germany, makes hafte to attack Paris. The King and Queen return thither with their army, and after various negociations the Prince is conftrained to depart. The two armies march towards Normandy—a memorable battle is fought at Dreue, where the Prince of Conde is made prifoner by the Catholics, and the Conftable by the Hugonots. In the firft onfet of this action, Gabriel of Montmorency, the fon of the Conftable, had been killed, the Comte of Rochefort had been thrown from his horfe, and loft his life, and the catholics, in fpite of all their bravery, began to give way. The German cavalry armed with piftols, and divided into two large fquadrons, having joined the Admiral in this critical moment, made a frefh charge with fuch fury, that they broke the Catholics, and forced them to fly. The Conftable who fought in this place with great bravery, exerted himfelf in vain to ftop and rally the fugitives : His horfe fell under him, and he was wounded in the left arm, furrounded by the Germans, and made prifoner, after having feen perifh at his fide, the Duke of Nevers, and feveral other officers of diftinction.

The Prince of Conde, in charging the cavalry of the Duke of Guife, was afterwards wounded in his right hand, and covered over with blood, and duft and fweat, was made prifoner by Daniville, who, wifhing to avenge the capture of his father, fought with defperation. The Duke of Guife remained mafter of the field of battle, the baggage and artillery of his enemy. The Prince

of

of Conde was brought into the prefence of his conqueror, and it was a memorable fcene to fee thofe two famous men, whom paft events, and efpecially the laft battle, had rendered implacable enemies, reconciled at once by the caprice of fortune, fup at the fame table, and for want of other lodgings, and better accommodations, pafs the nighi in profound fleep, on the fame bed.

Thofe who firft fled from this action, carried to Paris the firft news of the defeat and captivity of the Conftable, and threw the Court into deep mourning and great inquietudes. They were diffipated however, a few hours afterwards, by the Captain of the King's guards being difpatched by the Duke of Guife. The news which he fpread, and the affurances which he gave of the victory gained by the Catholics, diminifhed the grief caufed by the death of fo many brave men, whofe lofs had put all France in mourning. Befides the Lords and Knights, of diftinguifhed nobility and reputation, they reckoned eight thoufand men among the flain. The Duke of Guife acquired a glory without bounds by this victory, which gave a great check to the Hugonots. The King and Queen declared him General of the army, and he took the rout to Orleans, that he might not leave his enemy the time to repair their loffes.

No.

No. 28.

THE fiege and defence of Orleans, may be a good lecture on the military art, but is not directly to our purpofe, which at prefent is only to relate the fortunes and cataftrophes of the great actors in thofe fcenes of emulation, which have been before defcribed. There was in the party of the Hugonots, a gentleman, named Poltrot, of an active mind and a defigning character. He had lived fome years in Spain; and having afterwards embraced Calvinifm, and refided fome time at Geneva, he difcovered fo much zeal for his new faith, and entered with fo much zeal into all the intrigues of the party, that the Calvinifts in general confidered him, as a perfonage capable of attempting in their favor the moft hazardous enterprizes. It is not one of the leaft evils of a civil war, that no man's character is fecure againft fufpicions and imputations of the moft enormous crimes. It is almoft the univerfal practice for each party to charge the leaders of the other, with every bafe action, every finifter event, and every high handed wickednefs, without much confideration or enquiry, whether there is truth, or evidence, or even color to fupport the accufation. The Catholics pretended that the Admiral and Theodore Beza, engaged Poltrot to affaffinate the Duke of Guife, by promifes of great rewards, and by perfuading him that he could do nothing more acceptable to God, than to deliver his people from their moft cruel perfecutors. Poltrot yielding to their inftigations,

tions, pretended to have abandoned the Calvinift
party, and threw himfelf into the royal army,
where having infinuated himfelf into the houfe
of the Duke of Guife, he watched for a favorable
moment to execute his defign. The 24th of
February, 1513. the Duke after having given his
orders for an affault which he intended to make
the next day, at the bridge of Orleans, returned
at night to his quarters about a league diftant
from the trenches ; Poltrot, mounted on a Spanifh horfe, very fleet, waited for him, on his paffage, and feeing him accompanied, only by a gentleman of the Queen, with whom he was clofely
engaged in converfation, he fhot him in the back,
with an arquebufe, loaded with three balls. The
Duke was without arms, the three balls ftruck
him under the right fhoulder and pierced him
through the body ; he fell from his horfe for
dead.   His gentlemen, who marched before, that
they might not interrupt his converfation, returned, at this accident, and carried him to his
lodgings, where as foon as they had examined
his wound, his life was defpaired of. The King,
the Queen Mother and all the Lords in the army,
at the news of fo fatal a difafter, haftened to the
Duke's lodgings ; but all their cares and remedies were ufelefs ; he died in three days, with
great fentiments, fays Davila, of piety and religion, difcovering in his difcourfes a greatnefs of
foul and a moderation moft admirable. This
Prince, united with the higheft valor and fingular abilities, a confummate prudence. As profound in council, as active in execution, he always faw his defigns crowned with the happieft
fuccefs. Thefe qualities had procured him the
reputation of the firft Captain of his age, and his
                                    exploits

exploits merited the title of the defender and
protector of the Catholic religion. He left a
name glorious and celebrated to posterity, *tar-
nished however to endless ages with the just imputation
of intolerance.*

Poltrot had escaped into a neighboring forest ;
but tortured by the remorse of his conscience,
and by the terror of being pursued on all sides,
he wandered all night in the woods, without being able to find the road to Orleans. The next
morning, exhausted by fatigue, he was arrested
by some Swiss guards and led to the Queen and
the principal officers of the army. He alternately
accused and acquitted, both on the rack and at
his execution, the Admiral and Theodore Beza,
who published declarations throughout all Europe, denying in the most solemn manner, their
knowledge of the design of Poltrot. The court
hastened the execution of this monster, before
an opportunity had been given to confront and
examine him, as the Admiral requested, by quar-
tering him between four horses. The consequence was that the suspicion was fastened, on
these two austere and excellent characters, in the
minds of the Catholic party, though they have
been uniformly acquitted by the whole impartial
world. In consequence of the prejudices of the
Catholics, the children of the Duke of Guise pre-
served a cruel resentment, and took a horrible
revenge.

The death of the Duke of Guise was followed
by a general peace—and the Royal Army retakes
Havre de Grace from the English. The King arrives at his fourteenth year, and is declared of
age. The Queen's inventive genius imagines various means of appeasing the discontented Princes ;

ces ; and to accomplifh her defigns, travels with
the King through all the provinces of the kingdom. In Dauphiny they contrived an interview
with the Duke of Savoy ; at Avignon, with the
Minifters of the Pope ; and on the frontiers of
Guienne with the King and Queen of Spain.
To thefe Princes they might communicate their
fecret defigns, without apprehenfion of their
coming to the knowledge of the Hugonots,
which would have been almoft inevitable, if they
had employed Ambaffadors. The Queen, with
her ufual diffimulation, endeavored to prevent
the public from fufpecting her genuine defign,
and fecret views. She pretended that it was a
fimple defire in the King to fee his kingdom,
and fhow himfelf to his people. The Queen pretended to confent to it only to difplay before the
eyes of the people the magnificence of her court,
and to fee her daughter the Queen of Spain. Under the veil of thefc appearances, fo different
from the truth, nothiug was feen but magnificent preparations and fumptuous liveries—nothing was talked of but huntings, balls, comedies
and feafts. The interviews and intrigues in the
courfe of their journey with the Dukes of Lorrain, of Wirtemberg, and other Chiefs of the
Proteftants or Catholics in Germany ; the Count
Palatine, the Duke of Deux Ponts, the Duke of
Saxony, and Marquis of Baden, the Duke of Savoy, and the Minifters of the Pope, we pafs over.
In 1565, at Bayonne, they met the Queen of
Spain, accompanied with the Duke of Alva and
the Count de Benevent : While they pretended
to be there wholly employed in feafts and pleafures, they held fecret councils in concert, to
abolifh the diverfity of religion. The Duke of
Alva.

Alva, a man of a violent character, whose very name, as well as that of the Cardinal de Lorrain, is associated in every mind with bloody bigotry and anti-christian intolerance, said boldly, that to cut the root of all novelties in matters of religion, it was necessary to " cut off the heads of the poppies"—" To angle for the large fish—not amuse themselves with the frogs"—" When the winds shall cease to blow, the waves of the populace will soon be calmed." These are the miserable maxims of tyranny, whether it be exercised by a single man or a multitude. " There is no difference," according to Aristotle, and history and experience, " between a people governing by a majority in a single assembly, and a Monarch in a tyranny ; for their manners are the same, and they both hold a despotic power over better persons than themselves. Their decrees are like the other's edicts—their demagogues like the other's flatterers."—*Aristotle's Politics* Lib. 4. ch. 4.

Old Tarquin would not utter these maxims in words to the messenger of his son from Gabii, but walked out into his garden and struck off the heads of the tallest poppies with his staff. With no better authority than these trite aphorisms of despotism, did the Duke of Alva support his dogmatism, that a Sovereign could do nothing more shameful or contrary to his interests, than to grant to his subjects liberty of conscience, and his advice to employ fire and sword, to exterminate the Chiefs of the Hugonots.

No. 29.

THE Queen-Mother had either more hypocri-
fy, or more foftnefs of temper, or more cunning.
She was for effaying all means of alluring the
Chiefs of the Hugonots to the bofom of the
Church, and their obedience to the King.

The differences of circumftances, of manners,
of interefts and characters, as ufual, divided their
fentiments, and, caufing them to look at things
on different fides, dictated oppofite refolutions.
The two Kings however take meafures in concert
to fupprefs rebellions. The Queen of Navarre
comes to court. The King engages the family
of the Chatillions to a reconciliation with that of
the Guifes. Their reciprocal hatreds foon rekin-
dle and break out afrefh. The Queen of Navarre
in difcontent quits the court.

The advice of the Duke of Alva was conformable to the temper and character of this King.
He faid he highly relifhed the fentiment of the
Duke of Alva ; that the heads of thofe rebels
were too high in the State. The four families
of Bourbon, Montmorency, Guife and Chatillion,
all ftimulated by other fubordinate families de-
pendent on them, continue their emulations,
fallacies, hatreds, envies, oppofitions, intrigues,
manœuvres, combinations, decompofitions, tergiverfations : Another civil war breaks out, the
hiftory of which with its caufes and events, we
fhall leave the reader to read in detail. In 1567,
at the battle of Saint Dennis, the Conftable de
Montmorency, in fpight of five wounds he had

K e   received

received in the head and face, fought with extreme valor, endeavors to rally his troops, and
lead them on to battle, when Robert Stuart, a
Scot, came up to him and prefenting to him a
piftol, the Conftable faid to him, " you are ignorant then that I am the Conftable." " It is
becaufe I know you, faid Stuart, that I prefent
you this," and at the fame time fhot him in the
fhoulder with his own piftol ; although the violence of the blow ftruck down the Conftable, he
had ftill ftrength enough left to ftrike Stuart in
the face with the hilt of his fword, which remained in his hand, though the blade was broken, with fuch force as broke his jaw, beat out
three of his teeth and brought him down by his
fide half dead. The Hugonots were defeated
however, but the next day the Conftable died
at the age of forefcore, after having fhewn in
the action as much enterprize, bravery and vigor
as if he had been in the full ftrength of his youth.
He preferved to his laft moment, an admirable
firmnefs and prefence of mind ; a prieft approached his bed, to prepare him for death ; the
Conftable turned to him with a ferene countenance, and prayed to be left in repofe—adding,
it would be fhameful for him to have lived eighty
years, without learning to die for half an hour.
His wifdom, his rare prudence, and long experience in affairs procured for him and his family
immenfe riches, and the firft employments under
the crown : But he was always fo unfortunate in
the command of armies, that in all the enterprizes where he had the command in chief, he was
either beaten, or wounded, or made prifoner.

The Calviniftic army retired into Champaine,
and afterwards into Lorrain to meet the troops
they

they expected from Germany. The Queen, whom the death of the Conftable had now delivered from the power and ambition of the Grandees, and who remained the fingle arbiter of the Catholic party, would no longer expofe herfelf to the dangers of an unlimited power by advifing the King to name another Conftable or General of the army. She judged more proper to referve to the difpofition of the King and in her own power, the whole authority of the command. She therefore perfuaded Charles, by many reafons, to place at the head of his army, the Duke of Anjou, his brother, a young Prince of great hopes, but who was not yet fixteen years of age. The army is reinforced by fuccours fent from Flanders by the King of Spain, and from Piedmont, and many other places. The Duke of Anjou follows the Hugonots, to give them battle before their junction with the Germans. He overtakes them near Chalons : But the mifunderftandings and other obftacles excited in his council, hinder him from hazarding a battle. The Calvinifts pafs the Meufe and form a junction with the auxiliary troops commanded by the Prince Caffimir. They return into Champaine. The Queen goes to the army to extinguifh the divifions that reign there. They take the refolution not to attack the Hugonots, now become too formidable : but to draw out the war, into length ; marches off the two armies, fatisfied with obferving each other's motions. This Fabian fyftem of the Catholics difconcerts the Prince of Condé and the Admiral, unprovided with money to fupport, for any length of time, their army. In order to draw the royal army to battle they form the fiege of Chartres. The danger of that
city

city gives occaſion to new propoſitions of peace :
Indeed a peace is concluded and the two armies
are ſeparated ; but the Hugonots did not ſurren-
der all the places they were maſters of, nor did
the King diſcharge his Swiſs or Italian troops—
which occaſion new quarrels.

The court, ſeeing that the Hugonots did not
execute the conditions under which they had
been promiſed an oblivion of the paſt, attempts
to take off the Prince of Conde and the Admiral,
who had retired well accompanied, to Noyers in
Burgundy. They are advertiſed of their danger
and eſcape to Rochell, reaſſemble their forces,
and make themſelves maſters of Saintonge, Poitou and Tourdine. The King orders the Duke
of Anjou to march againſt them. The two armies meet at Janſeneuil, without engaging : they
meet again at Loudun ; the rigor of the ſeaſon
prevents a battle. The exceſſive cold obliges
them to march at a diſtance from each other.
Diſtempers break out in both armies and carry
off vaſt numbers. They open the next campaign
in the month of March. The Hugonots paſs the
Charente, break down the bridges, and guard all
the paſſages the Duke of Anjou, by the means
of a ſtratagem, paſſes the river. The battle of
Jarnac enſues. On the ſixteenth of March, 1569,
this famous action, ſo fatal to the Proteſtant
cauſe and to liberty of conſcience in France, as to
have annihilated, or at leaſt to have oppreſſed
both for two hundred and fifty years, took place.
The young Duke of Guiſe diſtinguiſhed himſelf
on that day, by attacking the left wing of the
Calvaniſts, commanded by the Admiral and Dan-
dilot at the head of the nobility of Britanny and
Normandy, and gave proofs of a courage, and
                                                        talents

talents capable of performing as much good, or committing as much evil as his father had done. The Prince of Condé, who commanded the main body, oppofed to the Duke of Anjou, fupported with intrepidity the fhock of the enemy, and when abandoned by his right and left, charged on all fides by the conquerors and furrounded by a whole world of enemies, he and thofe who accompanied him, fought with defperation. In arranging his fquadrons, he had been wounded in the leg by a kick of the Duke de la Rochefoucault's horfe, and in the combat his own was killed and overthrown upon him. This Prince, thus dangeroufly wounded, put one knee to the ground and continued to fight, until Montefquiou, Captain of the guards of the Duke of Anjou, fhot him through the head with a piftol. Robert Stuart, who had killed the Conftable at the battle of St. Dennis, and almoft all the gentlemen of Poitou and Saintonge, were cut in pieces, by the fide of the Prince.

The Duke of Anjou, fought in the firft ranks of his fquadron with a valor above his years, had an horfe killed under him, and ran great rifques of his life. The Hugonots loft near feven hundred noblemen or knights of diftinction. The foldiers, in derifion, with fcoffs and infults, bro't the body of the Prince of Condé upon an afs or pack-horfe to the Duke of Anjou at Jarnac.

> L'an mil cinq cens foixante & neuf
> Entre Jarnac & Chateau—neuf
> Fut porté mort fur une ăneffe,
> Le grand ennemi de la Meffe.

Young Henry, Prince of Navarre, begged the body of the Duke of Anjou, who fent it to Vendome

dome to the tombs of his anceftors. Thus lived
and died Louis ot Bourbon, Prince of Condé,
whofe valor, conftancy and greatnefs of foul, diftinguifhed him above all the greateft Princes and
moft famous Captains of his age. I fhall reverfe
the reproarhes of Davila, and fay that he deferves
to be cannonized as one of the proto martyrs to
liberty of confcience, inftead of that croud of
bloody tyrants with which the calender has been
difgraced.

The affairs of the Hugonots were in a critical
fituation. It was not doubted but that, after the
death of the Prince, the Admiral would be chof-
en for their Chief, both becaufe of the diftinguifhed employments which he had held in the
party, and the reputation which his prudence
had acquired. After the battle of Dreux, when
the Prince was made prifoner, the whole party,
with unanimous confent, had deferred to Coligni
the honour of the command. But at prefent
there were feveral gentlemen, who, by their
birth, their riches, or their other qualities, tho't
themfelves not his inferiors. Some of thefe tore
his reputation with flanders ; fome detefted the
aufterity of his character, *manners* and *habits.*
Unhappy Admiral ! thy fortune however is not
fingular. Merit, talents, virtues, fervices, of the
moft exalted kinds, have in all ages been forced
to give way, not to family pride, for this alone
would be impotent and ridiculous, but to the
popular prejudice, the vulgar idolatry, or the
fplendor of wealth and birth, with which family
pride is always fortified, fupported and defended.
The Admiral had loft, by malignant fevers, his
brother Dandelot and his friend Boucard : deprived of thefe two, the party which interefted
itfelf

itfelf in the grandeur and elevation of the Admiral, was confiderably weakened. But Coligni furmounted all obftacles by his addrefs—he began by renouncing in appearance thofe chimerical titles with which a vain ambition would have been fatisfied, propofing however, in fact, to preferve all the authority of the command. He refolved to declare Chiefs of the party and Generals of the army, Henry Prince of Navarre, and Henry Prince of Condé, fon of the deceafed Prince. During the childhood of thefe, the Admiral remained neceffarily charged with the conduct and adminiftration of all affairs of importance. It was, among Proteftants, as well as Catholics, in the caufe of liberty as well as that of tyranny, the only means of repreffing the ambition and pretenfions, the envy, jealoufly, malignity and perfidy of the grandees ; the only means of anfwering the expectations of the people, and of uniting minds which the diverfity of fentiment had already very much divided.

In this refolution, without demanding what he felt, he could not obtain—The Admiral intreated the Queen of Navarre to come to the army, reprefenting to her that the moment was arrived for elevating the Prince her fon to that degree of grandeur for which he was born, and to which fhe had long afpired. The Queen was not wanting in courage or fortitude : already refolved at all hazards to declare her fon the head of the party, fhe came with all the diligence which a ftroke of fo much importance required, and appeared with the two Princes at the camp at Cognac. Difcord reigned in the army, notwithftanding the neceffity of union and unanimity, to fuch a degree that it was on the point of difbanding. The

The Queen of Navarre, after having approved the views of the Admiral, affembled the troops; fhe fpoke to them with a firmnefs above her fex, and exhorted all thofe brave warriors to continue conftant and united, for the defence of their liberty and their religion. She propofed to them for Chiefs the two young Princes, who were prefent, and whofe noble air interefted the fpectators; adding, that, under the aufpices of thefe two young fhoots from the royal blood, they ought to hope for the moft happy fuccefs to the juft pretenfions of the common caufe. This difcourfe animated the courage of the army, who appeared to forget in an inftant the chagrin caufed by the lofs of the battle, and by the diffentions which had followed it. The Admiral and the Earl of Rochefoucault were the firft to fubmit, and to take an oath of fidelity to the Princes of Bourbon; the nobility and all the officers did the fame, and the foldiers, with great acclamations, applauded the choice which their Generals had made of the Princes for *Chiefs and protectors of the reformed religion.* This in human imaginations is confidered, and in human language is called, DIGNITY! The greateft Statefman, and the greateft General of his age, muft refign the command of his own army, even in the caufe of religion, virtue and liberty, to two beardlefs boys, becaufe they had more wealth, and better blood.

Henry of Bourbon, Prince of Navarre, aged 15, had however a lively fpirit, a great and generous foul, and difcovered a decided inclination for war : animated by the councils of his mother, he accepted without hefitation the command of the army, and promifed the Hugonots, in a

concife

concise military eloquence, to protect their religion, and to persevere in the common cause, until death or victory should procure them liberty.
The Prince of Condé, whose tender age permitted
not to express his sentiments, marked his consent
only by his gestures. Thus the Prince of Navarre, who joined to the superiority of age the
prerogative of first Prince of the blood, became
really the head of the party. In memory of this
event, the Queen Jane caused medals of gold to
be struck, which represented on one side her own
bust, on the other that of her son, with this in-
scription—PAX CERTA, VICTORIA INTEGRA, MORS
HONESTA—*A safe peace, compleat victory, or honor-
ble death.*

Coligni remains charged with the conduct of
the war, by reason of the youth of the Princes—
he divides his troops, and throws them into the
cities which adhered to him. The Duke of Anjou pursues his victory, and forms the siege of
Cognac, which he is obliged however to raise, by
the vigorous resistance of the besieged : he takes
several other cities. A new army of Germans,
commanded by the Duke of Deux Ponts, enters
France to assist the Hugonots. Wolfang of Bavaria, Duke of Deux Ponts, excited by the money
and the promises of the Hugonots, with the aid
of the Duke of Saxony and the Count Palatine of
the Rhine, at the solicitation of the Queen of
England, had raised an army of 6000 infantry,
and 8000 horse. In the same army was William
of Nassau, Prince of Orange, and Louis and
Henry his brothers, who, after having quitted
Flanders, to avoid the cruelty of the Duke of
Alva, supported the interests of the Calvinists of
France, whose religion they professed. This ar-

my

my marches towards the Loire, takes La Charite,
and paffes the river. The Duke of Deux Ponts
dies of a fever, and is fucceeded in command by
Count Mansfield. The Princes, and their Mentor
the Admiral, march to meet this fuccour. The
Duke of Anjou, for fear of being furrounded by
thefe two armies, retires into Limoufin. The Hugonots, combined with their allies, follow the
royal army. A fpirited action at Roche-Abeille.
The fterility of the country forces the Hugonots
to retire. The Queen-Mother comes to the camp.
The refolution is taken to feparate the royal army, to leave the forces of the Hugonots to con-
fume by time : it is feparated, in fact, and the
Duke of Anjou retires to Roches in Touraine.

No. 30.

THE Hugonots lay fiege to Poitiers. The Duke
of Guife refolves to throw himfelf into it to fuccour the garrifon. This young Prince, the object of the hopes of the Catholics, propofed to
himfelf to become one day their chief, by imitat-
ing thus, at the beginning of his career, by an
illuftrious and memorable example, the glory of
his father ; who, by the defence of Metz againft
the forces of the Emperor Charles the Vth. had
prepared his way to the higheft power and moft
brilliant reputation.

The Duke of Anjou propofes to raife the fiege
by a diverfion—he affembles his army, and leads
it to Chatelleraud. The Admiral raifes the fiege
of

of Poitiers, and obliges the Duke of Anjou to raife that of Chatelleraud. The Duke of Guife, however, by his activity in defence of Poitiers, and his frequent fallies, came out of it covered with glory and applaufe ; the whole Catholic party began to confider him as the fupport of religion, and the worthy fucceffor of the power of his father. Sanfac in vain lays fiege to la Charite. The Earl of Montgomery defeats the Royalifts in Bearn, furrounds Terfide, and takes him prifoner. The Duke of Anjou comes to Tours, to confult with the King his brother, and the Queen-Mother : The Duke of Guife came there alfo, fhining with honor and glory for the great actions by which he had fignalized himfelf at the defence of Poitiers. They all deliberated on the means of pufhing the war, and the Duke of Guife, coming in the place of his father, was then admitted for the firft time into the fecret council : he owed this favor to the fplendor of his birth, to the fervices of his father, to his own valor, to the protection of the Cardinal of Lorrain his uncle, but above all to the implacable hatred which the King had conceived againft the Admiral. After the death of the Prince of Condé, at the battle of Baffac, Charles had entertained hopes that the Calviniftical party, no longer fupported by the authority of a Prince of the blood, nor of a General capable by his reputation and his valor of fupporting the weight of fo great an enterprize, would feparate and difperfe, or at leaft incline to fubmit. But he faw, on the contrary, that the policy of the Admiral had reanimated the forces of his party ; that his valor and his ability, by availing himfelf of the name of the two young Princes of the blood royal, had
preferved

preferved union among the Calvinifts, caufed greater commotions, and expofed the State to dangers more terrible than any which had been before experienced. He therefore caufed the Admiral Coligni to be declared a rebel. by an arret of the Parliament of Paris, which was publiſhed and tranſlated into feveral languages. They dragged him in effigy upon an hurdle, and attached him to a gibbet in the place deſtined to the execution of malefactors : they ordained that his houfes fhould be razed to the foundations, and his goods fold at auction. From this time the King refolved to purfue the Admiral to death, began to elevate and favor the houfe of Lorraine, and above all the Duke of Guife, who, burning with ardor to avenge the death of his father, did not diffimulate the implacable hatred he bore to Coligni. The Admiral continues the war with vigor. The Duke of Anjou, whofe army, had been reinforced, feeks a battle : the Admiral endeavors to avoid it. At length he prepares for it, forced by a mutiny of his own army who demand it : he endeavors neverthelefs to retire : the Duke of Anjou purfues him, and joins him near Moncontour : the two armies come to action on the plains of Moncontour, and a bloody battle enfues ; victory remains to the Duke of Anjou, with a great carnage of the Hugonors. The party is difcouraged ; but the Admiral, although dangeroufly wounded, raifes their fpirits, and perfuades them to continue the war. The Princes and the Admiral abandon the whole country, except Rochelle, Angoulême, and Saint Jean d'Angeli.

Their defign was to join the Earl of Montgommeri—a refource which fortune feemed to have referved

referved to re-eftablifh their forces and repair their loffes. After that junction, they intended to remain in the mountains until the Princes of Germany and the Queen of England fhould fend them fuccors. They founded, moreover, fome hopes on the Marfhal of Damville, Governor of Languedoc, who for fome time appeared inclined in their favor, and with whom they maintain a fecret intelligence. While the Conftable lived, Damville had held a diftinguifhed rank in the Catholic party, and had fhewn himfelf a declared enemy of the Hugonots. His jealoufy againft Francis of Montmorenci, his elder brother, who was connected in friendfhip with the Prince of Condé and the Colignis, his relations, had infpired him with this hatred of the Calvinifts ; which had been fomented by the efteem which the Guifes profeffed for him, and the favors they procured him. Able and profound in diffimulation, according to conjunctures, they had employed all poffible artifices to retain him in their party, and by his intervention to attach to them indiffolubly, the Conftable, who difcovered much predilection and partiality for Damville, whom he believed fuperior in courage and abilities to his other children. The Queen-Mother made him the fame demonftrations. Obliged, during the minority of the King, to manage the grandees, fhe employed the Marfhal Damville to preferve her the attachment of the Conftable ; but after his death, all thefe motives and confiderations ceafed. The Queen, who had no longer occafion for Damville, gave herfelf little trouble to reward his fervices. The Guifes, far from fhowing him the fame regard, employed the management and perfuafions of the Cardinal of Lorraine,

Lorraine, who was now very highly in favor with Charles IXth. to deprefs and differve the Marfhal, as a fprout of an houfe which had been long the object of hatred and jealoufy to that of Lorraine. Damville foon perceived this change : the death of his father put an end to his differences with his elder brother, who was not lefs exafperated than himfelf at the refufal of the office of Conftable, poffeffed fo long by their father, and which they had folicited more than once. He began to make advances to the friends and relations of his family, and fought to renew an intercourfe with the Admiral, to whom he intimated fecret, though uncertain hopes. This motive had hindered him from fuccouring Terfide in Bearn, and from taking from the Hugonots the places which they held in Gafcony and Languedoc. He was the more inclined in favor of the Calvinifts, as he faw the Admiral already advanced in years, and every day expofed to evident dangers. If this nobleman fhould die before the Princes were of an age to command, Damville hoped to fucceed him in the command of the Calviniftic party :—finally, he dreaded, that if the King and the Guifes fhould overbear the Princes, the Admiral and all the Hugonots, they would then turn their efforts againft the family of Montmorenci, which would remain alone of all the ancient rivals, who had infpired him with jealoufy. Thefe difpofitions did not efcape the penetration of the Admiral. Excited by fuch hopes, he perfuaded the Princes to abandon the flat country, and retire with a fmall number of troops into the mountains of Gafcony and Languedoc. The Duke of Anjou befieges and takes Saint Jean d'Angeli, and lofes much time and many

many foldiers : he falls fick and retires firft to Angers, and then to Saint Germain. The Princes join the Earl of Montgommeri, and reinforce their troops in Gafcony. They pafs the winter in the mountains, and defcend into the plains in the fpring : they pafs the Rhone, and extend themfelves into Provence and Dauphiny. They march towards Noyers and la Charité, with the defign to approach Paris. The King fends againft them an army under the command of the Marfhal de Coffé, a general of little activity, and who defired not the ruin of the Hugonots. From a fear of confiding his armies to noblemen, whom their elevation, their power and their animofities, or the great numbor of their partizans, had rendered fufpected by him, the King committed the conduct of it to a General, who, perfifting in his ordinary inclination, gave the Hugonots a favorable opportunity to revive. This refolution was alfo attributed to the policy of the Duke of Anjou, who dreaded that fome other General might take away the fruit of his labors and victories. It is pretended that fuch motives engaged him to infpire the King with fufpicions againft all the other Princes and Generals, and to prefer, to them, a man whom he confidered as incapable of gaining any great advantages.

No.

No. 31.

═══

"Patrum interim animos, certamen regni, ac cupido verfabat."

THE two armies met in Burgundy—but the Princes, being inferior, evaded an engagement.

The Queen-mother, in 1570, had too much penetration not to unravel the manœuvres of the Marfhals de Coffé and Damville. She informed the King of them, and perfuaded him to liften to propofitions of accommodation. She perceived that the paffions and the perfidy of thefe grandees, might throw the ftate into the greateft dangers, if the war was continued. She was ftill more determined by the news which fhe received from Germany, where the Prince Cafimir began to raife troops in favor of the Hugonots. The finances were exhaufted to fuch a degree, that they knew not where to find funds to pay the Swifs and Italian troops, to whom they owed large arrears. In fhort, they wifhed for peace ; and were weary of a war which held all men's minds in perpetual alarm, which reduced a great part of the people to beggary, and which coft the ftate fo many men, and fo much money. The King held, with the Queen-mother, the Duke of Anjou, and the Cardinal of Lorraine, councils, in which they refolved to return to the projeƈt, already fo many times formed and abandoned *to grant peace to the Hugonots—to deliver the kingdom from foreign troops, and finally to employ artifice, and take advantage of favorable conjunƈtures—to take off the chiefs of the party, which they thought would yield of itfelf, infallibly, as foon as it fhould fee itfelf*
deprived

deprived of the support of their leaders. It was thus, that the court would have fubftituted *craft* inftead of *force*, to execute a defign, which the obftinacy of the Hugonots, or the want of fidelity in thofe who commanded armies, had always defeated when recourfe had been only to arms.

With fuch dark and horrid views were overtures of peace made, and conditions concluded. The Princes and Admiral, ftill diffident and diftruftful, retire to Rochelle. The King endeavors to gain their confidence. To this end, he propofes to give his fifter Marguerite in marriage, to the Prince of Navarre, and to make war in Flanders upon the Spaniards. The marriage is refolved on, and all the Chiefs of the Hugonots come to Court. The Queen of Navarre is poifoned. After her death the marriage is celebrated, during the feafts of which, Admiral Coligni is wounded by an affaffin. The King takes the refolution that, as in extreme cafes it is imprudence to do things by halves, the Hugonots fhould be exterminated. The night between the 23d and the 24th of Auguft, 1572, a Sunday called Saint Bartholomew's Day, the Admiral is maffacreed, and almoft all the other Calvinifts are cut in pieces in Paris, and in feveral other cities in the kingdom.

Such, in nations where there is not a fixed and known conftitution, or where there is a conftitution, without an effectual balance, are the tragical effects of emulation, jealoufies and rivalries—deftruction to all the leaders—poverty, beggary and ruin to the followers. France, after a century of fuch horrors, found no remedy againft them but in abfolute monarchy : nor did any nation ever find any remedy againft the miferies of fuch rivalries among the gentlemen, but in defpotifm, monarchy, or a balanced conftitution. It is not neceffary to fay, that every defpotifm

G g   and

and monarchy that ever has exifted among men, arofe out of fuch emulations among the principal men ; but it may be afferted with confidence, that this caufe alone is fufficient to account for the rife, progrefs and eftablifhment of every defpotifm and monarchy in the four quarters of the globe.

It is not intended at this time to purfue any further this inftructive though melancholy hiftory, nor to make any comparifons, in detail, between the ftate of France in 1791, and the condition it was in two or three centuries ago. But if there are now differences of opinion in religion, morals, government and philofophy—if there are parties, and leaders of parties—if there are emulations—if there are rivalries and rivals —is there any better provifion made by the conftitution to balance them now than formerly ?— If there is not. what is the reafon ? who is the caufe ? All the thunders of heaven, although a Paratonnere had never been invented, would not in a thoufand years have deftroyed fo many lives, nor occafioned fo much defolation among mankind, as the majority of a legiflature in one uncontroled affembly may produce in a fingle Saint Bartholomew's Day.* Saint Bartholomew's days are the natural, neceffary and unavoidable effect and confequence of diverfities in opinion, the fpirit of party, unchecked paffions, emulation and rivalry, where there is not a power always ready and inclined to throw weights into the lighteft fcale, to preferve or reftore the equilibrium.

With a view of vindicating republics, commonwealths and free ftates, from unmerited reproaches, we have detailed thefe anecdotes from the hiftory of France. With equal propriety we might have reforted to the hiftory of England, which

---

* Upon Franklin's authority, the French adopted their government in one affembly.

which is full of contefts and diffentions of the fame fort. There is a morfel of that hiftory, the life and actions of the protector Somerfet, fo remarkably appofite, that it would be worth while to relate it—for the prefent however it muft be waved. It is too fafhionable with writers to impute fuch contentions to republican governments, as if they were peculiar to them; whereas nothing is further from reality. Republican writers themfelves have been as often guilty of this miftake, in whom it is an indifcretion, as monarchical writers, in whom it may be thought policy; in both however it is an error. We fhall mention only two, Machiavel and de Lolme. In Machiavel's hiftory of Florence, lib. 3, we read, " It is given from above that in all republics, there fhould be fatal families, who are born for the ruin of them; to the end that in human affairs nothing fhould be perpetual or quiet."

If indeed this were acknowledged to be the will of heaven, as Machiavel feems to affert, why fhould we entertain refentments againft fuch families? They are but inftruments, and they cannot but anfwer their end. If they are commiffioned from above to be deftroying angels, why fhould we oppofe or refift them! As to " the end" there are other caufes enough, which will forever prevent perpetuity or tranquility, in any great degree in human affairs. Animal life is a chemical procefs; and is carried on by unceafing motion. Our bodies and minds, like the heavens, the earth and the fea, like all animal, vegetable and mineral nature; like the elements of earth, air, fire and water, are continually changing.— The mutability and mutations of matter, and much more of the intellectual and moral world, are the confequence of laws of nature, not lefs without our power than beyond our comprehenfion. While we are thus affured that in one fenfe no-

thing

thing in human affairs will be perpetual or at reft ; we ought to remember at the fame time, that the duration of our lives, the fecurity of our property, the exiftence of our conveniences, comforts and pleafures, the repofe of private life, and the tranquility of fociety, are placed in very great degrees, in human power. Equal laws may be ordained and executed, great families as well as little ones, may be reftrained. And that policy is not lefs pernicious than that philofophy is falfe, which reprefents fuch families as fent by heaven to be judgments : It is not true in fact. On the contrary they are fent to be bleffings—and they are bleffings until by our own obftinate ignorance and imprudence, in refufing to eftablifh fuch inftitutions as will make them always bleffings, we turn them into curfes. There are evils it is true which attend them as well as other human bleffings, even government, liberty, virtue and religion. It is the province of philofophy and policy to increafe the good and leffen the evil that attends them as much as poffible. But it is not furely the way, either to increafe the good or leffen the evil which accompanies fuch families, to reprefent them to the people as machines, as rods, as fcourges, as blind and mechanical inftruments in the hands of divine vengence, unmixed with benevolence. Nor has it any good tendency or effect, to endeavour to render them unpopular ; to make them objects of hatred, malice, jealoufy, envy, or revenge to the common people. The way of wifdom to happinefs is to make mankind more friendly to each other. The exiftence of fuch men or families is not their fault. They created not themfelves. We, the Plebeians, find them, the workmanfhip of God and nature like ourfelves. The conftitution of nature and the courfe of providence has produced them as well as us :

and

and they and we muſt live together; it depends on ourſelves indeed whether it ſhall be in peace, love and friendſhip, or in war or hatred. Nor are they reaſonably the objects of cenſure or averſion, of reſentment, envy or hatred, for the gifts of fortune, any more than for thoſe of nature. Conſpicuous birth is no more in a man's power to avoid, than to obtain. Hereditary riches are no more a reproach than they are a merit. A paternal eſtate is neither a virtue nor a fault. He muſt nevertheleſs be a novice in this world who does not know that theſe gift of fortune, are advantages in ſociety and life, which confer influence, popularity and power. The diſtinction that is made between the gifts of nature and thoſe of fortune appears to be not well founded. It is fortune which confers beauty and ſtrength, which are called qualities of nature as much as birth and hereditary wealth, which are called accidents of fortune: and on the other hand it is nature which confers theſe favours, as really as ſtature and agility.

Narrow and illiberal ſentiments are not pecular to the rich or the poor. If the vulgar have found a Machiavel to give countenances to their malignity, by his contracted and illiberal exclamations againſt illuſtrious families, as the curſe of heaven: the rich and the noble have not unfrequently produced ſordid inſtances of individuals among themſelves, who have adopted and propogated an opinion that God hates the poor, and that poverty, and miſery on earth are inflicted by Providence in its wrath and diſpleaſure. This noble philoſophy is ſurely as ſhallow and as execrable as the other Plebeian philoſophy of Machiavel; but it is countenanced by at leaſt as many of the phenomena of the world. Let both be diſcarded as the reproach of human underſtanding, and a
diſgrace

difgrace to human nature. Let the rich and the poor unite in the bands of mutual affection, be mutually fenfible of each others ignorance, weaknefs and error, and unite in concerting meafures for their mutual defence, againſt each other's views and follies, by fupporting an impartial Mediator.

That ingenious Genevan, to whom the Engliſh nation is indebted for a more intelligible explanation of their own conſtitution than any that has been ever publiſhed by their own Acherly or Bacon, Bolingbroke or Blackſtone, has quoted this paſſage of Machiavel, and applied it, like him, to the diſhonour of republican governments. De Lolme, in his conſtitution of England, Book 2 c. 1. fays—" I cannot avoid tranſcribing a part of " the fpeech which a citizen of Florence addreſſed " once to the Senate : the reader will find in it " a kind of abridged ſtory of all republics." He then quotes the paſſage before cited from Machiavel.

Why fhould fo grave an accufation be brought againſt republics ? If it were well founded, it would be a very ferious argument, not only againſt fuch forms of government, but againſt human nature. Families and competitions, are the unavoidable confequence of that emulation, which God and nature have implanted in the human heart, for the wifeſt and beſt purpoſes, and which the public good, inſtead of cooling or extinguiſhing, requires to be directed to honor and virtue, and then nouriſhed, cheriſhed, and cultivated. If fuch contentions appeared only in republican governments, there would be fome color for charging them as a reproach to thefe forms ; but they appear as frequent and as violent in defpotifms and monarchies, as they do in commonwealths. In all the defpotifms of Afia and Africa, in all the monarchies of Europe, there are conſtant fucceſſions of

emulation

emulation and rivalry, and confequently of contefts and diffentions among families.   Defpotifm,
which crufhes and decapitates, fometimes inter-
rupts their progrefs, and prevents fome of their
tragical effects.   Monarchies, with their fpies,
letters de catchet, dungeons and inquifitions,
may do almoft as well.   But the balance of a free
government is more effectual than either, without any of their injuftice, caprice or cruelty.
The foregoing examples from the Hiftory of
France, and a thoufand others equally ftriking
which might be added, fhow that Bourbons and
Montmorencies, Guifes and Colignis, were as fatal families in that kingdom as the Buondelmenti
and Huberti, the Donati and Cerchi, the Rici
and Abbizzi, or Medici at Florence.

Inftead or throwing falfe imputations on republican governments ; inftead of exciting or fo-
menting a vulgar malignity againft the moft refpectable men and families—let us draw the proper inferences from hiftory and experience—let
us lay it down for a certain fact, firft, that emulation between individuals, and rivalries among
families, never can be prevented : fecond, let us
adopt it as a certain principle that they ought
not to be prevented, but directed to virtue, and
then ftimulated and encouraded by generous applaufe and honorable rewards.   And from thefe
premifes let the conclufion be, as it ought to be,
that an effectual controul be provided in the conftitution, to check their exceffes and balance their
weights.   If this conclufion is not drawn, another will follow of itfelf—the people will be the
dupes, and the leaders will worry each other and
the people too, till both are weary and afhamed,
and from feeling, not from reafoning, fet up a
mafter and a defpot for a Protector.   What kind
of a Protector he will be, may be learned hereafter from Stephen Boetius.

POSTSCRIPT.

IF any one wifh to fee more of the fpirit of Rivalry, without reading the great Hiftorians of France, he may confult L'Efprit de la Ligue-L'Efprit de la Fronde and the Memoirs of De Retz and his Co-temporaries. The hiftory of England is more familiar to Americans ; but, without reading many volumes, he may find enough of Rivalries in thofe Chapters of Henry's hiftory of Great Britain, which treat of civil and military affairs. If even this ftudy be too grave, he may find, in Shakefpeare's hiftorical plays, efpecially Henry 4th, 5th and 6th, and Richard the third, enough to fatisfy him. If the gaity of Falftaff and his affociates, excite not fo much of his laughter, as to divert his attention from all ferious reflections, he will find, in the efforts of ambition and avarice, to obtain their objects, enough of the everlafting pretexts of religion, liberty, love of country and public good, to difguife them. The unblufhing applications to foreign powers, to France, Germany, the Pope, Holland, Scotland, Wales and Jaok Cade, to increafe their parties and affift their ftrength, will excite his indignation : while the blood of the poor cheated people, flowing in torrents on all fides, will afflict his humanity.

The Englifh Conftitution, in that period was not formed. The houfe of Commons was not fettled ; the authority of the Peers was not defined ; the prerogatives of the Crown were not limited. Magna Charta, with all its confirmations and folemnities, was violated at pleafure, by kings, nobles and commons too. The Judges held their offices at pleafure. The Habeas Corpus was unknown ; and that balance of paffions and interefts which alone can give authority to reafon, from which refults all the fecurity to liberty and the rights of man, was not yet wrought into the Englifh Conftitution, nor much better underftood in England than in France. The unity of the Executive power was not eftablifhed. The National force in men and money was not in the king but in the landholders, with whom the kings were obliged to make alliances in order to form their armies and fight their enemies foreign and domeftic. Their enemies were generally able to procure an equal number of powerful Landholders with their forces to affift them, fo that all depended on the chance of war.

It has been faid, that it is extremely difficult to preferve à balance. This is no more than to fay that it is extremely difficult to preferve liberty. To this truth all ages and nations atteft. It is fo difficult, that the very appearance of it is loft, over the whole earth, excepting one Ifland and North-America. How long it will be before fhe returns to her native fkies, and leaves the whole human race in flavery, will depend on the intelligence and virtue of the people. A balance, with all its difficulty, muft be preferved, or liberty is loft forever. Perhaps, a perfect balance, if it ever exifted, has not been long maintained in its perfection ; yet fuch a balance as has been fufficient to liberty, has been fupported, in fome nations, for many centuries together ; and we muft come, as near as we can, to a perfect equilibrium or all is loft. When it is once widely departed from, the departure increafes rapidly, till the whole is loft. If the people have not underftanding and public virtue enough, and will not be perfuaded of the neceffity of fupporting an Independent Executive Authority, an Independent Senate and an Independent Judiciary power, as well as an Independent Houfe of Reprefentatives. All pretenfions to a balance are loft and with them all hopes of fecurity to our deareft interefts ; all hopes of Liberty.

51884

DATE DUE